INTIMATE STRANGERS:
TRUE STORIES FROM QUEER ASIA

Edited by Gregg Schroeder
and Carmen Ho

FOR RAMLEEN

♡ ♡ ♡

Nancy L. Conyers :)

XO

4/8/20

Signal 8 Press
Hong Kong

Intimate Strangers:
True Stories from Queer Asia

Editors: Gregg Schroeder and Carmen Ho
Published by Signal 8 Press
Copyright 2019 Gregg Schroeder and Carmen Ho
ISBN: 978-988-77949-4-3

Ansh Das Media Ltd
Signal 8 Press
Hong Kong
www.signal8press.com

Cover design: Manuela de Gioia
Art direction: Cristian Checcanin

CONTENTS

INTRODUCTION

WHEN I was invited to be a co-editor of this anthology with Gregg, I was thrilled to have such a rare opportunity, but I was also unsure how it would turn out. I had no idea what kind of submissions we would receive and whether we would even have enough stories to publish within our timeframe. LGBTQ+ writers are already a minority, let alone those from or who have lived in Asia and want to write creative nonfiction in the English language. The enthusiasm we received was therefore inspiring and unexpected. The fifteen stories here document with poetry and precision the lives of LGBTQ+ people in a part of the world that is in many ways hostile to them—places that are slowly becoming more progressive but which are still cruel and dangerous for those who don't fit into society's perceived sexual and gender norms. These stories are important literary works from courageous writers who, by speaking up and sharing their experiences, are giving a voice to a community that needs to be heard and seen.

Perhaps the most heartwarming quality of this collection is the undeniable resilience and fighting spirit that shines through despite the difficulties, pain, and loneliness evident in the stories. I say *fighting spirit* because for LGBTQ+ people, especially in many parts of Asia, being ourselves is indeed a fight—a constant battle. One part of the battle is, of course, sharing your true self with people at the risk of losing friends and family. In "All the Ways to Say I'm Gay," Aaron Chan shows how coming out is not a single act but an ongoing process, something that needs to be done over and over again in different contexts. Dear reader, if you are a straight ally wondering what the big deal is, please consider how Aaron's question "Do you still love me?" is a very real question many LGBTQ+ people have for their parents. For them, the need to ask such a heartbreaking question is a reality. The relief and gratitude LGBTQ+ people feel when we are accepted by family is as liberating as taking a breath of air after almost drowning.

Edward Gunawan explains in "Crows Like Us" that because of the difficulties we face, LGBTQ+ people respond to stressors such as job losses, breakups, and grief over lost loved ones more adversely. Statistics from around the world show that LGBTQ+ people are often targets of violence, discrimination, and marginalization, leading to a high rate of depression and suicide. "A correlation, however, does not equate to causation. Being LGBTI is not a precursor to suicide," Edward writes. Indeed, the systemic problems that create such correlation are external factors, which is perhaps why LGBTQ+ people around the world have been migrating and living transnational lives, in search of freedom from cultural expectations. Yet, for Asians, moving to more liberal countries in the West often brings the challenges of being a racial minority in a "pre-dominantly white gay culture." This intersection of sexuality and ethnicity is an important topic to discuss, and Edward's piece provides personal insights that many Asians would find relatable. In "My Divine Comedy," Agatha Verdadero talks about a quest of a similar yet different nature. She travels far from home but finds her home within, her sanctuary in God: "I found my peace and joy as a pilgrim in a foreign country on the day I prayed."

Family, love, friendship, acceptance—none of these pillars of happiness are certainties for LGBTQ+ people. And when the society at large tells you that you should not be who you are, knowing and loving yourself can be a long and arduous journey. In "Does Your Name Make You Gay?," Huang Hai-su shares how growing up she was told to use a "gay-proof" name. Krista Melgarejo discusses in "Banyo" the frustrations that come with navigating gender expectations, and the pressure to be exceptional in order to be treated with respect if your identity is considered unconventional. Dating is a whole other challenge for LGBTQ+ people in Asia: Alistair Yong says in "Gift from God" that finding a life partner is "a rarity in this part of the world." Indeed, I also feel that it is nothing short of a miracle, and thought, as he once did, that "love in all its forms did not exist in the community." Fortunately, these stories show us that this is not true at all. Sometimes you just have to look around the corner; perhaps like Simon Wu, who didn't know he "grew up just round the corner from the only gay bar and disco in Hong Kong," you will one day look back on your life and see how, as he describes in "Kaleidoscope," the seemingly disconnected fragments fall into place to create a beautiful pattern. Some nights may seem never-ending, but as Beatrice Wong so beautifully states in "From Beavis (M) to Beatrice (F)," in crowded cities "it's so dense that it's hard to not bump into hope."

The shared hope in these stories is a beacon of light. For LGBTQ+ Asians who have to navigate the traditions and social expectations of their cultures, harbouring any hope at all is in fact a profound act of rebellion against oppression. The stories between these pages are therefore part of a revolution, a transnational movement for equality. "Fighting back is necessary," Ingvild Solvang says in "L for Latitude," and while foreign residents who advocate for LGBTQ+ rights in Asia play an important part in this movement too, it is, as Ingvild powerfully illustrates in her piece, the locals who are at the front line. Her story also shows how progress is not a given; if people allow and endorse narrow-mindedness, cities that are known for their tolerance can also become fertile grounds for hate and bigotry, as in the case of Yogyakarta which at the height of political tension was "decorated with anti-LGBT banners." This is a reminder of the importance of activism, whether through politics, education, art, or other ways of expanding minds and fostering empathy. Like the LGBTQ+ supporters in Yogyakarta who have continued to stand firm despite the negative turn, we must work together to build compassionate, safe, and inclusive societies that celebrate diversity.

So, dear reader, I hope these stories, which we are so proud of, bring you a sense of unity, belonging, and empowerment. Whether you're in the mood for a lighthearted read or a serious discussion, you'll find what you're looking for in this collection; you'll be laughing and crying and perhaps punching the air with renewed energy through it all. On lonely days,

I hope these stories also remind you that you are never alone. And if you know anyone who might appreciate these stories, please share. In Ingvild's words, "Taking care of each other is the most powerful act of resistance." So let's be here for one another. Let's thrive together.

Carmen Ho
Co-editor

S EXUAL minorities slalom between expectations and obstacles on the way to achieving personal goals while staying within the norms of the particular society in which we live. For some, that wavy course still includes feigning heterosexuality or otherwise negotiating compromises with the authentic self. Others find ways to glide delicately around social rules to achieve what's right for them without upsetting the heterosexual hierarchy. Still other LGBTQ+ pioneers turn their backs on cultural expectations and lawful practices entirely, creating their own domestic ecosystems. Psychologists tell us the drive to conform is powerful, and so we persevere each in our own way in the face of resistance, even when flight may seem more sensible than fight. The desire to belong—to love and make love, to form bonds, to create a family—is among the strongest motivators for human beings. Love and acceptance are among our very basic needs.

In the eastern reaches of Asia—where most of the fifteen writers collected here come from or write about—fitting in and finding love and intimacy is notably harder for the LGBTQ+ community than for our straight relations. Times and mores are changing, but rights remain limited: Eight of the nineteen territories in the region have protections for sexual minorities on the books at this writing, but same-sex sexual activity is illegal in five others, including parts of Indonesia and all of Malaysia. (Interestingly, in Singapore sexual activity between consenting men is against the law; for women, it is not.) No territory allows same-sex couples to adopt children outright. Laws concerning gender identity and expression are more progressive, with legislation in place in at least eleven territories allowing trans people to register their gender changes, though most are permitted only after reassignment surgery. Japan, Taiwan, and Cambodia recognize same-sex relationships in some jurisdictions. Not one of the countries or territories recognizes same-sex marriage.

In this vast and complex matrix of societies, cultures, histories, values, expectations, and languages, a common thread can be found linking LGBTQ+ people: finding ways to create safe zones to fit into this rich range of social settings; living life on authentic terms.

*

The pieces in *Intimate Strangers* are all concerned with creating a place and belonging. These are personal stories by and about people who devise their own custom-made spaces in which to live and thrive. Sometimes, making room for a new way to live that feels right means taking small steps to accommodate the realities of people and place. Beijing writer Ember Swift, in "A 'Grandparrot' Performance," declares:

I am the foreign daughter-in-law who now lives separately from [the mother- and father-in-law's] son in a dynamic that the older Chinese generation cannot begin to wrap their heads around. We aren't together, but still married. There are many reasons for that for now, but namely, big changes must be made gradually for me here—the foreigner in a foreign land. Legal footing is flimsy. Flirt with fear to keep it at bay.

As Germaine Trittle P. Leonin of the Philippines explains in the title piece, "Intimate Strangers," sometimes praying for a partner can bring surprises, and it's necessary to make room for the unexpected:

> She once told me that she had only asked God to give her someone who is kind, patient, understanding, and loving. She had always assumed God would take care of the gender requirement, so maybe it was her fault for not being more specific.

The dreaded discomfort of not fitting in cannot be managed from the sidelines. An attempt to join the fray must be made—and sometimes the result is a thing unexpected and beautiful. Hayley Katzen discovers herself to be lithe and flexible, once she takes the plunge—figuratively as well as literally—dancing with domestic helpers on their day off in Hong Kong in "A Common Language":

> I join the back row, mirroring their movements and suddenly in my thick-soled runners and shapeless shorts I am graceful and soft and flowing. Now the voice from the speakers snake-charms my body. Now, alongside women whose names I don't know, where our common language is dance, where there's no innuendo or expectation, where the fans are my only partner, I sway and step.

*

Social and cultural barriers are real enough. But legal restraints call for their own zigzagged course to subvert officialdom. The practical difficulties in confronting systems where same-sex relationships are not recognized are challenges that Nancy L. Conyers and her wife learn to navigate from Shanghai and Hong Kong to Singapore, but never really get used to, as she explains in "'Are You Married?' Is Not a Yes or No Question":

> Even though China was the most fascinating place we've ever lived and Shanghai is the most incredible city in the world where my heart will continue to live for the rest of my life, the stress of having to be closeted took its toll. We, of course, didn't keep completely quiet and made decisions about who to tell and who not to tell, but now that we're not there anymore I realize the day-to-day anxiety I lived with. Every time there was an unexpected knock at the door, I jumped.

And then there are our own expectations—what internal barriers to love we set and what we allow ourselves to get away with. Colum Murphy finds that making space for love doesn't just need a public cover story to deflect those who are nosey and judgmental after he relocates to China. He needs a reason that will convince himself, too, as he explains in "Rough Like Velvet":

> I came here for love. But I was damned if I was going

to come to Guangzhou only for a relationship. So, I enrolled in a year-long Chinese course, where I would have to explain myself anew, this time to a motley cohort of language students.

Couples do succeed, and relationships can be long lasting regardless of legal status. Some partners find the best way for them to manage non-recognition is not placing importance on the institution of marriage at all. The practicalities, for the most part, can be worked around by other means, as Jenna Collett discovers in conversation with a pair from the Philippines in "In Defence of Dyke Shirts (and Marriage Equality)":

> "Twenty-seven years. No marriage." The phrases are uttered toughly. "Why would we get married? We can go to Cali and get married. We can go to Canada and get married. For what? For face? We'll get no recognition, no security, no property. I'm sixty-fucking-four. Why must I marry for face? I have a house. I've got a lawyer. The papers don't say married, but she gets my house. She'll get everything."

A lawyer's work makes for a surrogate marriage, when that's the best that can be done.

*

It has been a rare honor to co-edit this anthology with Carmen, not only for the chance to collaborate on a collection of works by underrepresented voices, but also to get to glimpse through the many windows opened wide by each of the writers whose creative view of his or her world is showcased here. It's up to all of us as readers and writers, voyeurs and exhibitionists, to seek out one another, support one another, read and listen to and discuss one another's point of view, and to make space for each other's experience.

We hope you enjoy this collection.

Gregg Schroeder
Co-editor

Editors' note

ENGLISH is used by 20 percent of the world's population—around 1.5 billion people—in a colourful range of varieties. As such, a wide spectrum exists from the various standard to vernacular styles. In celebrating each writer's story in *Intimate Strangers*, we aimed to preserve the language choices of the individual writers, with some practical concessions to unify the entire collection. Join us in celebrating the variety and richness of English as it is used throughout the Asia-Pacific region.

MY DIVINE COMEDY

By Agatha Verdadero

"YOUR sister said you're a lesbian. Are you?"
My next heartbeat was light years away as I
stood petrified at your bedroom doorway. Your
shrunken frame barely filled the white Monobloc chair you
sat on, but your presence permeated everywhere. Your wedding portrait—with the floral lace of your trousseau and veil
in delicate pointillist detail on the canvas—leaned against
a corner. Rosary beads peeked from under a pillow. A stack
of adult diapers sat on upright luggage along one side of the
room. An electric fan revolved at promenade pace overhead—
perhaps because the AC was too cold for your bones. Curtains
were drawn shut to keep the piercing sun at bay, away from
your sensitive eyes. This was your territory and I was a tres-
passer, hovering over the threshold.

Though I towered over you, I almost cowered in fear at
being ambushed. I had just landed at midnight from a six-
teen-hour journey across two continents, weighed down by a
welcome from strangers who, at various stations, stamped my
passport, sold me a local mobile phone SIM card, and drove
me to a friend's condo, where I was to stay alone, in the middle of the country's central business district. Unlike so many
other arriving Filipino passengers with their families' ecstatic

messages writ bold on placards by the exits, I had nothing, not even a cup of tepid coffee, to mark my homecoming. My eldest sister didn't send her driver to pick me up this time. And never will again, she said.

After a night of fighting for sleep against urban noises and jet lag from my eyrie high above the metropolitan grid, my alarm clock ordered me to stumble onto a bus close to scorching noon to have lunch with you as the foremost order of the day. I had headed back to see you because you said, "I can't hold on any longer," several months ago. You had to see me in the flesh one final time. I was grateful you waited for me while I wrapped up some urgent work matters because my secret terror was for you to depart in my absence. You never hinted then that you had a burning question that needed to be asked before I could even step into your room.

"So, are you?"

I could have stammered through a lie, but you did not suffer liars gladly. In my childhood, you gave me the impression that the ridges between your brows could slice through any fog of deceit I surrounded myself with. When you cast that furrowed glare my way, it was easier to admit that the Dutch milkmaid figurine had slipped through my fingers while dusting the shelf and shattered to pieces on the floor than to mutter a denial, even when I knew the inevitable spanking would follow. Your hand was an anvil. Before I had reached third grade, I already understood what a Napoleon complex was because Dad somehow had to explain through my tears how you managed to bring down a broom handle or a rubber slipper so hard across the back of my thighs. It wasn't a thorough explanation, as far as I was concerned, but it had to do.

You were the eldest among eight siblings, but even then, all of them stood above you in adulthood. Before you turned ten, you had already notched a few life-and-death runs through pitch-dark rice fields during the Second World War while intermittent gunfire between Japanese occupying forces and Filipino guerrillas punctuated the night, just to fetch the midwife from the next town for the arrival of a new brother, a new sister. You were a parent to them even before you had a chance to play with a real doll, which was non-existent in a time of war. Perhaps it's because you grew up at light speed and bore grave responsibilities at an early age that you brooked no childishness from your own daughters.

"Yes, Mom, I am."

I choked on the last two syllables, not that they were untrue but because—suddenly—I could breathe again. "I am" pealed in my mind like a carillon. My utterance to you of the truth was the release I never knew I needed. I gasped and my lungs quickly filled with life, astonished at the purity of oxygen after at least two decades of vacuum. This must have been what I felt when I was born blue in the face, with my umbilical cord around my neck. The surgeon could not have freed me from that stranglehold fast enough, when I bawled my entry into the land of the living. It cost you a scar on your belly and meant any future childbirth had to follow suit.

As I celebrated freedom within, I tightened my knees instinctively. I braced myself for the inevitable rage, scanning your face warily for the telltale twitches at the corners of your mouth and eyes, portents of doom as when I went below an

A in any subject at school. You held your stare straight at me while swaying to the internal metronome of your resting tremors. Your seventy-six years sloped your shoulders, but everything else about you and the room was undisturbed. Your hands were at peace on the armrests.

"When Dad was still alive," you began.

My jaw dropped a fraction. I had expected a maelstrom, but your voice was a gentle breeze crossing the breach between us. And I was confused. Dad had died in 2007. What part did he play this very moment? I was ready to doubt your remembrance of things that had transpired more than six years ago, as a defence against the inevitable verbal whiplashes. I held my breath again, but I saw your eyes brighten at the memory. Luminescence was not an attribute I associated with you.

"He and I talked…"

I took it for granted I would be fodder for conversations in your empty nest. As the youngest among three daughters, I appeared to be the errant one, having transplanted myself nine thousand kilometres away from home in 2002. I had given up my tenure as assistant professor "to work among refugees" from the Horn of Africa and the Great Lakes Region. In my oversimplified paradigm then, that meant teaching them their ABCs and the English language, to prepare them for their relocation to various parts of the Northern Hemisphere.

When I said goodbye to you and Dad, I explained my uprooting as divine will, derived from prayer and reading God's word. I did not delude myself into thinking I was saving people. That is God's province. I had enough difficulty saving pesos and dollars to afford the six-month Swahili language studies required of incoming long-term volunteers. I went simply because, as I always said to my elder sister, "God determines the times and spaces we occupy." He said go, so I went. There was no parting of clouds, no clap of thunder, no mandate carved on stone by an invisible hand. Whatever He wanted to do with my life while I was in Africa, I trusted He would show me. I have always believed God's work focused on the unseen things. It is not ever captured as a photo-op or a sound bite or a video clip for followers of social media to devour.

"We both agreed, no matter what happens…"

In the next few years, we became strangers to one another. From the briefest of emails and phone calls, I gathered that you and Dad had increased your number of maintenance drugs to keep blood clots from forming, bones from breaking, and hearts from bursting. I would have wanted to know more about the minutiae of your days in our home at the foot of an active volcano, but I felt I had no right to ask. I was the one who had chosen to set down roots away from you, halfway across the world. I had to live with the consequence of not knowing anything current about family. *Hivyo ndivyo ilivyo.* It is what it is, in the language of my adopted land.

So when the rare phone call or email happened, I delivered my own vanilla narrative: I was safe behind the electrified fences and guarded gates of Nairobi's leafy (read: upscale) suburbs, conveniently forgetting to share that I once almost lost my mobile phone to a teenage snatcher in a school uniform, had my screeches for help not summoned nearby masons and plumbers from their construction sites. They had collared him and he tumbled into an open ditch, where they proceeded to introduce him to the tools of their trade with which they had armed themselves, despite my renewed screams—this time, for them to stop the lynching playing out for a small crowd of gathering oglers. The young man was finally able to run away, leaving behind only a torn notebook in the trench, slowly bleeding black ink as it absorbed the flowing water.

I chose to regale you instead with stories about waking up to hyaena and elephant tracks outside my tent in Amboseli and triumphing against the wind shear at four thousand nine hundred metres above sea level to reach Point Lenana and stand above the clouds. They were the reports you wanted to hear because they painted the Africa promised by the pages of old *National Geographic* issues we bought from the dry section of Central Market. So while your news of ailing health struck fear in my heart at the shortness of your days, I convinced you that my new home indeed offered a fabulous, unending safari every day, bookended by oranges at dawn and maroons at dusk.

"We will love whoever you love. We just want you to be happy."

And it was that declaration that shook me to my very foundation. Because in spite of my silence, my avoidance of mention, You. Knew. You both knew that I had a different voyage, the real voyage, going on in my interior landscapes, not through scree or savannah. In the intervening years especially since university, I had begun questioning who and what I saw in the mirror. I could not reconcile the woman who enunciated English words to South Sudanese children with the woman whose gaze lingered a little too long on Julia Roberts's face in *Mona Lisa Smile*. And why was it Elena who captivated me in *Cinema Paradiso*, not Salvatore? You and Dad brought me up according to a moralistic worldview, where absolutes existed because there is a God. I always felt I needed to kneel bare-skinned on mung beans to cleanse my soul every time I stared at the "wrong gender." I was too frightened to tell you about the second circle of hell I was going through as I struggled over identity. It had not just been a phase in my twenties when being part of an experimental theatre group and the cultural scene felt like an open licence for me to explore beyond the Michaels of my high school years.

When Dad died in his seventy-second year, I came home to your fading. You had a permanent hunch on your back. Your skin draped loose from your arms. You had more silver in your hair, which you did not even try to hide. And you had lost part of your voice. Your desktop computer was now forever shut down because you never learned to use it. Only Dad had the password to your joint email account. So, face to face, you and I tried to catch up on stories about how the grandchildren were growing up fast and how I had moved on from refugee work to start my own publishing house and consultancy. However, the one narrative I wanted to share I could not speak about because infernal fires were licking at my soles.

For me, it took four years, several thousands of Kenyan shillings for counselling, and a few life chapters before I found my peace and joy as a pilgrim in a foreign country on the day I prayed, "Lord, I really am attracted to other women and I don't know what to do about it. Please help me." With that surrender, I set about shedding four decades of pretence and concluding my own internal war. It was then that I found my sanctuary in God again. I was actually THE refugee who needed a home.

When I told my sisters about it, they affirmed their love for me. However, time told the true tale of two sisters: one fell silent; the other became incensed—"You dishonoured the family name"—and that seemed to result in my eldest sister's revocation of all courtesies towards me. I was in a spirit of disquiet about telling you because of their reactions. I feared your heart would stop, literally. As it turned out, in spite of assurances to spare you the truth, my estranged sister pre-empted my confession by telling you about it herself.

"Your dad and I both agreed, we will love whoever you love."

Two years after I was born, you gave birth to my brother. Sadly, we lost our healthy baby boy due to a negligent nurse who left him to drown from his milk bottle while she stepped out of the nursery to flirt with her visiting boyfriend and you were recuperating in your room after another C-section and a tubal ligation. If not for that surgery and the procedure, you wouldn't have stayed longer than usual that fateful week. Eleven years after Noel's brief life, in a fit of rage for a now-forgotten transgression committed by my adolescent self, you had shrieked, "I wish it were you who died in place of your brother."

From that point on, I had no expectations of us ever again finding ground to honour the wound on your belly from birthing me and the trauma that made me bolt upright from the littlest sensation of breathlessness. As far as I knew, I was your reject daughter, your constant reminder of what you had lost.

But now, across the span from the doorway to your chair, a new bridge had been built and I recognised it as the work of divine hands because only God could create something from the void. I took tentative steps towards you, mindful that the weight of the past had just gone; a new chapter had begun.

The curtains billowed in the wind and I could hear birds tapping on your windowpanes. My feet shuffled over to where you sat. I knelt down to embrace you, before I even realised that my face was wet with tears. Your arms were home and I was once again nestled under your beating heart. That instant, I understood what the salvation and love of Christ meant in their fullness and glory. There was divine grace enough to come back full circle to this.

I knew nothing about how you travelled from your severe persona to being just Mom that day, but I knew something about the transformative power of God-ordained passages. I had lived through my own. Sadly though, we never had the chance to explore the lost years fully—only that we each had the chance to ask each other for forgiveness. You died at the end of 2013. Our hours together in the last months of your life were always too short, too ridden with pains ravaging your physical body. Not even my hands could knead away your agony. But of this, I am certain: nothing of our history mattered anymore. In your final days, you gave me space to tell you about a woman I met. You listened and smiled. You held my hand. You kept me safe.

But already my desire and my will

were being turned like a wheel, all at one speed,
by the Love which moves the sun and the other stars.

—*Paradiso*, Canto XXXIII, lines 142–45, C.
H. Sisson translation

A "GRANDPARROT" PERFORMANCE

By Ember Swift

S HE is squawking and barking at once. She's like an indignant parrot that's been swallowed by an anxious Schnauzer dog. "She" is my mother-in-law. My Chinese mother-in-law.

I am the foreign daughter-in-law who now lives separately from her son in a dynamic that the older Chinese generation cannot begin to wrap their heads around. We aren't together, but still married. There are many reasons for that for now, but namely, big changes must be made gradually for me here—the foreigner in a foreign land. Legal footing is flimsy. Flirt with fear to keep it at bay. They're why.

My eyes find the heads of my two babies, now six and four, bent over their colouring books at their kids' table in the middle of my in-laws' tiny one-room apartment. The kids are the focal points of all four of us adults who live in this traditional Chinese apartment compound in Beijing in three different buildings. For the past nearly three years, I've been in building one on the far left of the compound. He's still in building eight on the far right. Symbolically, my in-laws live right in the middle, in building four. It's like a domestic teeter-totter, grandparents as fulcrum.

My mother-in-law's Shandong accent is sharp in my ears. Scratchy. I am actively soothing them with subtle deep breaths as I've always done. This is my tenth year here, so I'm used to this. Well, sort of. I have seen her emotional tsunamis before, which seem to be so acceptable in this culture, perpetuated by Chinese television that dramatizes all the spiraling and frothing that families do behind closed doors. The media demonstrates; the people mimic. I used to react to it, but that's a bit like a mountain trying to grow taller to brace itself against the tsunami when it hits: it doesn't work and you still get wet, and maybe even more so because the wave feels all the more challenged.

Anyway, she's raving about Chinese culture—something I'll never understand, apparently—but this time it's in protest to my having taken the kids for brunch with my friends and their twin two-year-olds. Her "problem" is that they're two men, a gay parental unit.

"Chinese culture doesn't support that." She practically sprays this with a righteousness that sticks to my nerves. "They're not a normal family!"

I sigh. "Those aren't my values. They're a different family, but they're still normal."

"We don't accept this in our country."

I am growing weary. She has already risen and walked the room twice. She repeats herself. She sits back down. She gets back up. She paces. I listen and contest quietly in the tiny spaces of time that become available for any retort. I repeat that it's important that the kids learn that there are all different kinds of families. I point out that ours is also different than most Chinese families because it's a cross-cultural family. She hears these words and swats them aside like they're just dizzy houseflies of annoyance.

The problem with this particular episode is the thickness of my skin. Or, should I say, the thinness of it. I am sensitive to that which judges or looks down upon not only my core community, but also my own personal identity.

You see, I have never come out to my mother-in-law. Or my father-in-law, for that matter. I am a proud queer woman and when I met my husband in 2007, he was a man across the room whom I first mistook for a woman. I was already in my early thirties and despite defining as "queer," an inclusive term that includes bisexuality, I had never fallen in love with a man before him. I got completely swept up in the romance of it all. It was a beautiful, swirling love affair that saw us married within eighteen months and then soon embarking on parenthood. The novel traditions also charmed me—the heterosexual and Chinese traditions both equally foreign to queer, Canadian me. So, eventually, coming out to my in-laws just seemed irrelevant. Besides, my personal sexual identity had always allowed for the occasional sideways glances at men, especially those with high cheekbones and long hair. (I'm a sucker for the pretty boys.) So, he didn't change my sexuality; he just broadened it. He knew I wasn't straight from the very beginning. I never will be.

Early on in our relationship, my husband told me that telling his parents wasn't necessary. "They wouldn't understand it. This isn't the West," he said. I respected his advice. "They're a product of the Cultural Revolution, after all. They're not open-minded."

I've come to believe that this might not be so true after all. You wouldn't know it from my mother-in-law's giant emotional wave right now, but my in-laws have more than accepted me as the foreign daughter-in-law. That's an open-minded act. They have also met many of my queer friends and their families. In fact, 80 percent of my community back home in Canada is queer-identified in some way: lesbian, trans, bi, gay, genderqueer, etc. That's the world I came of age in. And many of them have come to visit me in Beijing over the years. As this isn't an explicit culture, no friend's identity was directly discussed, per standard decorum, but I assumed an implicit awareness and acceptance.

"You shouldn't be teaching them that this lifestyle is acceptable," she says, her voice rising. The barking is itching my eardrum again, bird feathers catching in the throat.

"I don't agree. I'm teaching the kids that love is love, family is family," I say, forcing more calm. (Sometimes I worry that my calm is notably condescending, which might be fuelling the squawking. Hard to know.)

She tries a different tactic: "Aren't gay people just, what… 20 percent of the population?" she asks, not waiting for an answer. "So few! They're too young to have to be introduced to this. They don't need this education now. They might never meet gay people in their lives."

I am surprised by her logic. "Uh, it's more like 10 percent—"

"Even more reason to keep them away from it!"

"Again, I disagree. If in every ten people one is gay, they're definitely going to meet gay people. They might even be gay themselves! Ten percent is a lot of people in the world! But regardless of statistics, they need to learn acceptance, that the world isn't all the same…" (I pause, wishing I knew the Mandarin word for "diversity.")

"These are just your foreign ways. We are Chinese. We have to represent the Chinese ways. And, it's not okay. It's just not right." More sticky absolutism hits me in the face. I instinctively reach up and wipe my forehead.

"Look, Ma," I go on, addressing her with the familial word for mother, "imagine if one of our kids is gay. I mean, there's a 10 percent chance, right?" I gesture to the kids still colouring in this increasingly claustrophobic room. They shoot furtive glances up at us, my daughter especially anxious by the possibility that this is going to escalate into a bigger fight. She hates arguing. I'm sure this is a leftover stain from the often verbally explosive relationship I had with her father. The creases in her brow stab me with familiar regret. I soften my voice and say to my mother-in-law, "So, what if one of our kids turns out to be gay? If they know you feel this way about the gay identity—"

She cuts me off again, a verbal knife slicing through watermelon: "This is not something they should choose! It's not normal. It's not right!"

I bring my volume down yet another notch. "This isn't a choice, Ma." More softener. "It's an identity. People don't choose to be gay. It's not an easy life to be different." But I flip back to the scenario. "What if it's Little Dragon here?" I use my son's Chinese nickname. "If he knows these are your views then he will never tell his grandmother the truth about his life for fear of losing your love."

"I wouldn't accept it!"

New tactic: "What if it were your own son?"

"I wouldn't accept him. I'd abandon him. It's disgusting. It's wrong!"

Her pitch has flipped up yet again and I can hear the angles of sound tinkering metallically off the ceiling's corners. She's up from her seat again. She's paced across the room and is randomly adjusting something on a shelf that seems to be bothering her with its position, perhaps in the same way my argument is. Then she's back at the table. Sitting.

"If you had a choice to either accept your child or lose your child, I know you wouldn't choose to lose him."

"I'd lose him! I wouldn't want him this way! No way!"

I smile now. She is acting in a television drama. It's a fantastic performance. Her arms slashing the air with their emphasis, her face contorted, extremism the key ingredient. Like a parrot, she's in mimicry mode. Is this what she thinks she must model for the kids?

My father-in-law is sitting on a short stool off to the side and concentrating very hard on the sunflower seed dish in front of him, one by one, slowly transferring them to his mouth, extracting their empty shells from his teeth and forming a small hill on the kids' table to his left.

"Your father agrees with me!" she says, suddenly noticing her silent spouse, his head bowed. He glances up at me, anxiously mute.

I'm still smiling when I say, "As usual, you have a mouth like a knife and a tofu heart刀子嘴豆腐心." This expression is perfect for her. "I know you too well for that, Ma. You're too soft-hearted to abandon your loved ones!" I say this with lots of warmth in my voice, like I'm petting a small furry animal, and I know it's teetering on patronizing, but the affection in my tone is surely going to reach her. It's a wager.

I see my father-in-law stifle a grin at my use of the Chinese expression. Her fanfare flags. It's worked. I know full well that she loves these children of ours with an intensity that even she admits exceeds that with which she loves her own son, their dad. But this pause is short-lived. Once again, she refills her indignation and is up from her seat.

"Chinese people simply cannot tolerate such unnatural choices," she repeats, this time using more formal words. I can tell that I'm not going to win this argument with her tonight. I decide to give her a bit more personal insight.

"You know, my friends are a Chinese man and a British man. The Chinese man's mother and his auntie help them with the kids. They haven't been abandoned in the least. It seems that his Chinese family has more than accepted his identity."

She looks at me blankly. She registers their domestic scenario as a direct contradiction to what she is asserting—that all Chinese people of her generation would reject such a situation—but she can't allow me the victory. The loss of face alone is too much for her as the matriarch, I know this. So, I dutifully sweep in just in time.

"But everyone has their own opinion. I hear yours."

This conversation isn't going to resolve itself, and besides, it's almost time for me to take the kids home for bed. I lean back in my chair, and my daughter, Echo, chooses this exact moment to interject. She saves us more awkwardness.

"Stop fighting, Mommy," she says to me in English. I focus in immediately on her chocolate eyes.

"We're not fighting, honey. This is a discussion. Mommy and Nainai disagree about something, but it's an important subject and we have to talk about it. Don't worry, we're probably going to stop now. We have to go soon anyway." I say these words with a gentleness I usually reserve for their bedtime stories, but it seems needed now. My son, Topaz (Little Dragon) responds by putting down his crayons and wandering over to my knees to silently crawl into my lap. He is only four, but he heard his name mentioned earlier and I know he's been listening as closely as his sister. I cuddle him and kiss his head. I have two sensitive little pups.

My mother-in-law takes in all these cues like a pro, even though she doesn't understand our English. She lets the waves settle for the time being. Sitting in her chair across from me, she is leaning slightly forward and stiff, one hand flat on the glass surface of the dining table, the other on her knee. She looks poised to rise again but she doesn't. Her lips are tight.

"You know how I learned about this?" she asks in a more normal voice. I detect some conspiracy in her tone. "Your daughter! She told me about your friends and that you told her that when she grows up she can marry a boy *or* a girl— either would be fine! You can't tell her that kind of thing! It's not true. I told her 'that's ridiculous, you can't marry a girl!'"

I nod. "Yes, I said that."

It's true. I have been reinforcing the idea of equal marriage. It's my ethics. I will always impart my ethics to my children. That's called parenting. Besides, I have several married gay friends, including the friends with whom we had brunch.

"These kids can marry whomever they love," I add. I state this as fact. I'm using a new tone to convey that these are my immovable values. It was value differences I cited as the main reason for my split with her son, as well. And while they didn't really want details, I discovered that such a strong rationale was enough to silence further inquiries. So, I garnish this last point with simple words: "You and I clearly have some core value differences. But we will always be one family."

The layered impact of these words is tangible, but deflection is the Chinese way. Her eyes flash with an immediate understanding of why I have used them but she takes a hard left around their meaning. "Anyway, I would find out." (She's referring to my suggestion that her grandchildren wouldn't tell her about their lives.) "These days, everything you need to know about a child's life is on the Internet anyway!"

She adds a near-violent gesture toward the laptop at her left elbow, and it is then that I know, intuitively, as though it has long been her trump card, that the width of my sexuality was long revealed to her without my ever having to come out. I am a musician, after all. A musician with a public profile and, even though I also publicly married her son, my queer (or, with Chinese translation: bisexual) identity is surely traceable online in either language. And, she just used the typical roundabout Chinese way to tell me that.

Something inside of me twists uncomfortably.

My marriage couldn't have survived for a lot of reasons, but our different sexualities were not at the top of that list. In fact, I'm grateful to him for opening up my sexuality in such a way that now allows for love to exist with either gender, not just women. Now that I have experienced it with their son— and it was indeed a true love—there is no telling what genital apparatus will exist between the legs of the next person I fall in love with. For me, it's no longer important. But that back-flip in my belly tells me that perhaps they think I left him because I don't like men.

Enter that feisty fear.

If ever there were a custody battle in this country, I would lose. This advisory came directly from a Chinese lawyer. She explained that regardless of my involvement with my children and my capabilities as a wage earner, or my track record as a sound and loving mother, I have a few immediate strikes against me here. First of all, I'm a foreigner on a spousal visa, which means I'm not legally allowed to work here. I also have no assets. So a court battle would expose me as either an illegal worker or would implicate me as a non-wage earner with no assets to my name. Secondly, I am the female parent in a patriarchal culture that favours the "ownership" of children to the father's side. Thirdly, my in-laws are very involved in the children's lives, and my extended family is across the world; therefore, I have no support network "on my side." The kids would automatically be awarded to the father because of the grandparents, the lawyer told me. Add to the mix the fact that I'm not heterosexual, and homophobia forms the whipped cream on the loss-of-custody cake.

My daughter comes over and wants half of my lap. I say what I always say: "Good thing Mommy has only two kids because I have only two legs and two arms, one for each of you!"

I let her crawl up. My son begrudgingly gives way to his bigger sister. The kids are a bit whiny, surely in reaction to the energy in the room. My father-in-law finishes his sunflower seeds and looks up at my "curled-up puppy" lap with a smile.

"Anyway," she says, standing up with a sigh in her stance, "we don't agree. Let's talk about it some other time."

Those could have been my exact words. I'm elated that she's called a "time out." I'd rather not have such a sensitive and important conversation in front of the kids anyway, but it's too late for that. We need to go regardless and so we all shuffle off the chair and I get my kids into their coats for the short walk across the compound to my apartment.

"Thanks for the delicious dinner," I say to my mother-in-law.

"What are you thanking me for?" she says, as is her way. I'm not meant to thank family for the things that family does for family. Not in Chinese tradition. Nevertheless, it's my cultural way to express appreciation, so I do it instinctively. She knows I'll thank her and she likes the acknowledgement, but she'll dismiss my appreciation as inappropriate. In return, I like the acknowledgement of being family and not an outsider, even though I'm the foreign daughter-in-law, so I dismiss her refusal to accept thanks as irrelevant. In the end, even though it's never easy to bridge these cultural chasms, I really love these people.

The familiar "thank you" dance complete, we file out of their little apartment and say our goodnights. The sky is dark as we emerge from their building and snake our way between the other buildings back home. Two little hands are in each of mine. We are quiet for a few steps before Echo looks up and asks, "Mommy, can I still marry a girl even though Nainai says I can't?" Her eyes are clouded with worry.

"Echo baby, you can marry whomever you love, or you can also choose not to get married. But no matter what you choose, we will always love you." I decide to speak on behalf of the whole family. Even her Nainai.

A neighbour walks by us with a yappy brown dog. Its round face has a little underbite and it looks at us like a mini warrior. The kids instinctively veer away from its shrill bark in a protective half-circle, forever worried little dogs will bite them. That's probably well founded.

"Don't worry, guys, you're safe. This dog has more bark than bite," I say. *Like your grandmother*, I think to myself.

And then, out of the blue, my son asks me a question that makes me laugh out loud: "Mommy, can we have a bird that talks? My teacher says some birds can talk in *Engwish*. That dog only speaks dog *wanguage* but I want a bird that speaks *Engwish*." His absentee L's are so adorable that I want to squeeze him all over, not just his little hand as we walk.

I tell him that these are called parrots, but no, we can't get one because they're very expensive and we aren't going to be in China forever. He's a bit disappointed but he says, "Okay, then."

Besides, I think, *there's enough parroting happening in this culture without a real live one in our house!* Suddenly I see myself as the evil bird owner who grins with glee at the removal of a parrot's voice box, and this nearly makes me laugh out loud again. I bite my lip.

Oh China, I think, *you have darkened my humour.*

Kaleidoscope: Memoir of a Hong Kong Boy

By Simon Wu

THE first time I see two men making love, my whole body shakes uncontrollably and my whole world order shatters into a blizzard of multicoloured pieces and I wonder if I can ever put them back together again. It is 1985 and I am watching a film at a private residence in Causeway Bay, not a porno film, a German art film, *Taxi zum Klo* (*Taxi to the Toilet*). The film is being screened by Zuni Icosahedron, an avant-garde theatre company, at probably Hong Kong's first unofficial Gay and Lesbian Film Festival.

I am twenty-three and a virgin, just graduated from the University of Hong Kong, returning to live back home with my parents in Tuen Mun after three years of freedom living in Swire Hall, a newly built, squeaky-clean, featureless dormitory on the university campus—eight floors for boys, top two floors for girls. Two to a room, potluck who you get to share with—a dish or a troll. With a bit of plotting and skullduggery, I manage to share my room with my best friend, a boy I am hopelessly in love with. I am so mad about him that I even encourage him to date a girl I know is also secretly in love with him. That girl becomes his girlfriend. I boast that their love affair is entirely my creation. News about my Cupid role circulates around the dormitory, and before long my roommate and his girlfriend hear about it and are furious—my heartthrob decides to avoid me at all costs, and in a jealous rage I take a soft plastic figurine, a present to me from his girlfriend, cut it into a thousand pieces, and dump it in the rubbish bin in our room for him to see. Does he see it? I never find out because we never talk again. Two "strangers" sharing a room, it is a perfect hell.

At twenty-three, I am desperate for a man, any man, but I don't know where to find one—no Internet, no personal ads in newspapers, no mention of people like me at all anywhere. Homosexuality is a crime, maximum penalty life imprisonment. In the lift after watching *Taxi to the Toilet*, I exchange glances with a man. He follows me. He catches up with me while I'm waiting to cross a busy road and asks me to go home with him, to have a cup of tea. I agree. Little does he know how desperately I need that "cup of tea."

Disaster. I am so overwhelmed that I don't actually enjoy it. But I've done it, or rather, had it done to me. I am no longer technically a virgin. He has opened a door for me, a door that can never be closed again. He told me about a bar called Dateline, a disco called Disco Disco, both in Central, a short walk from my old home at Aberdeen Street—a dilapidated three-storey wooden building above Wong Lo Kat herbal shop. So I grew up just round the corner from the only gay bar and disco in Hong Kong. If only I'd known.

Red

One sunny day in 1966, I'm kicking my plastic football about in the street outside our building when I suddenly run up against two hairy columns rising up from a pair of worn-out rubber flip-flops: my father, back from the sea, and he's holding a massive box in his brown sinewy arms. A voice comes from behind the box: "Ah Kuen, get out of my way."

The box is so big it casts a shadow over me like a cloud. In the box is our first television set.

The other kids only see Santa once a year, but I see him twice. Whenever Dad comes back from a voyage, he always brings presents. This time it's a big one!

We are the first family in the entire building to have a television set, and we quickly become the centre of attention, our neighbours constantly popping their heads around our floral patterned curtain and goggling at the endless stream of monochrome programmes. The screen is fuzzy, full of "snowflakes," but this doesn't dampen their enthusiasm one bit.

Each night, the last thing I see on TV before transmission closes down is a photograph of the Queen, wearing her royal sash like Miss Hong Kong; my mother says the Queen is my godmother, and I believe her. I am so used to seeing her frozen in the photograph at the end of each day that I am shocked when I see a film of her moving, waving her hand from the balcony of a large building. Photos on the family altar are for you to worship, you don't expect them to move! Imagine your grandmother in the photo on the shrine waving at you. It's scary!

Things are going along just fine, and then my brother comes along. My parents are very happy and proud about his arrival; I am far, far less excited about him than I was about the TV. He's born on the Kitchen God Day in 1967.

I think my mother has indigestion, although how can she have indigestion without eating? And what's that got to do with the appearance of my brother? Shortly after the birth of my brother, they say streets are not safe and I am worried. They say people in the streets are waving little red books. What are the little red books? They say bombs are everywhere. What are bombs? Is my brother one of the bombs?

Madam Lau's eldest grandson, Ah Leung, is playing "Puff the Magic Dragon" on his record player when Mum brings the baby back home; but poor Peter, Paul, and Mary have no chance against my brother who is making more noise than all three of them put together. What really hits me is my brother's smell; it's like boiled lamb chops.

We share our cramped living space with the Lau family: Mr. and Mrs. Lau; Mr. Lau's widowed mother ("Madam Lau"); their four sons (Leung, Man, Ning, and Chung); Bro Lai ("Coming"), a bachelor in his late thirties; and Shuet Tze ("Auntie Snow"), a spinster in her fifties. There is a ladder next to our kitchen/toilet that leads up to a small dark space that Shuet Tze lives in; she is a cleaning lady, keeps herself very much to herself, and I tend to steer well clear of her twilight zone. My family lives closest to the kitchen; then, separated by a flimsy partition and curtain, are the Laus; and next to them, closest to the balcony, is bachelor Lai. A narrow corridor from the kitchen to the balcony runs by all these living areas.

The youngest of the Laus' sons, Ah Chung, lives in a makeshift area next to Auntie Snow, separated by a cardboard divider, accessible via a ladder through a trapdoor. This windowless area, lit by a single light bulb, is the secret headquarters of the boys where we gather to talk and play games. One day we're there playing cards; I am about seven at the time. Ah Chung takes out a magazine he found in Bro Lai's room and shows it to us. "Hey guys, look at this." Naked men and women, doing all sorts of painful things to each other! The boys get really excited, laughing, pointing, slapping their knees, making jokes about the women's breasts and the dark, flat V-shape between their legs. I am too shocked to join in. I sit there dumbfounded, appalled, and amazed at the gargantuan size of the men's erect members and the fuzzy mass of black hair at the base of them—this phenomenon is completely new to me. I can't imagine growing up to be like that. I think to myself, no way can that ever happen to me! Why does Coming Lai want to look at something horrible like this? The images from this porn magazine burn into my cortex and stay with me right through my childhood and adolescence.

The next penis I see is a few years later—a real one this time. I am dribbling a plastic football up the corridor next to where the Lau family live when, out of the corner of my eye, I see Ah Ning, the second son, stark naked, about to get dressed. I quickly dribble the ball around in a circle and kick it back down the corridor, which gives me the excuse to go past him again—too late, he has already put on his underpants. I feel a keen sense of disappointment and frustration. For some reason, after that, my eyes are always drawn to Ah Ning and my heart hops like a little sparrow if he is around.

The balcony is the most romantic place for me. It was originally rather shabby and could barely accommodate two people, but after the only renovation ever carried out in our building, the balcony was reinforced and slightly enlarged. I like to sit out there on my stool and watch the blurry head-lights of cars in the rain as they speed down our steeply slop-ing street, and sometimes, if luck is smiling, the shameless bone-setter in the building opposite who showers without closing the curtains. He lives on the second floor and I live on the third, so I can look down into his living area and see his naked bottom. I notice that he always showers around seven to eight in the evening and so I make sure I will be at the balcony at that time. The bone-setter is a slightly chubby guy with plump and juicy white buttocks; he never showers look-ing out the window, so I only see his back and bottom, never his penis. One day, I cricked my neck and my mum takes me to see him; seeing him close up, I decide that it is much better to keep my distance and let my imagination do its work while he is showering.

White

When a typhoon comes, the adults jump around, shouting, closing all the windows, sticking tape across the glass, putting out spittoons to catch the rain dripping from cracks in the ceiling, getting torches and candles ready for a blackout.

During a typhoon I love watching the waterfall that cascades onto our balcony from the lower end of the tilted tiled roof; I pull back the balcony stools one by one so they won't get wet, drawing out the drama of the rescue operation. As the water pours down from holes in the gutter, it hits the railings and splashes all over me. The other boys copy me and it turns into a game, each boy showing off his skills at rescuing stools from the torrents of rain. The excitement mounts, not because of the wind or rain, but because of the intense competition, each boy acting like a male peacock in the mating season. Tired of the stool rescue game, Ah Man, the third son of the Laus, runs into our communal kitchen for a pee; that's where we do it, on the kitchen floor, then flush it with water from an earthenware pot down the drainage hole. The night before the typhoon, dozens of cockroaches emerged from the drainage hole, crawling all over the kitchen, some of them even flying into our rooms. Ah Man, a sadistic bully, comes back with a paper bag full of these terrifyingly large cockroaches, intending to offer them to me, pretending they're sweets. But his evil plan comes to an abrupt end when typhoon signal nine is hoisted and we have to evacuate the building, fast.

As the wind and rain build up into a fury, we are sent to a modern concrete flat several blocks down the road, which is owned by the herbal tea shopkeeper from the ground floor of our building. With our mackintoshes and umbrellas, we rush down the steep, narrow wooden staircase. Some of the stairs have caved in and the light is dim, yet we don't need to see as we can feel the steps—our feet remember.

The street is completely deserted and the signboards swing dangerously to and fro. Everything is blurring white with blinding rain.

When we get to the herbalist's flat, all the boys are herded into a little room where they can be safely contained. All the windows are closed and sealed, and without adults and without anything to do, it is a perfect time for us to run loose. We wrestle with one another, desperate to pull each other's trousers down. We usually go for the bigger but weaker kids' trousers. At that age, we seem to be able to see through to each other's heart. We identify our prey by exchanging a few glances and then we all jump on him. We can feel the hot breath on our necks, we can smell sweat in the stuffy air, we can hear our hearts beating like bongos, and we can see our hands and legs all entangled together and our focus, of course, never leaves the trousers.

The wind is howling outside, the storm is upon us.

Blue

I love falling out of bed. With the arrival of my little brother, I move up to the top bunk of the double-tiered bed and, despite the rail, I also manage to fall down from up there. After this my mother thinks that it's better for me to sleep with her on the lower bunk bed until I'm older, so our bed is enlarged with the addition of several wooden planks which, to make space, have to be removed every morning. My mother sleeps in the middle between my brother and me. My father, a merchant seaman, is seldom at home.

When I'm twelve I have a strange dream—a man being

raped by a woman! I wake up with a jolt and find that I have wet myself! I tip-toe past my mother and brother (like a ninja on TV) to the chest of drawers where I get myself a fresh pair of underpants to change into. But why did I pee in my dream? And why is this pee so much stickier than the normal pee? Am I sick or something?

Months later, I secretly browse a neighbour's women's magazine, *Sisters*. In each issue, there are pink pages talking about sex—I come across the word "masturbation," which in Chinese literally means "lewd hand," and start to wonder—is this the reason for my sickness?

I begin to notice that my dreaming eye always focuses on the men—the women are mere shadows in the background. And this is the case when I graduate to pleasuring myself— the men are always the stars of the show I put on in my head. When it's over, I use the curtain next to my bunk bed to wipe myself clean. I find it's easy enough not to make any noise, but it's an art not to shake the bed. On the rare occasion when Dad's back from the sea and he's doing it with Mum, it makes it easier for me to do it in sync without anyone noticing.

The building is full of holes and everyone has their own particular way of filling them in. I fill in a hole in the kitchen door with my eyes. The kitchen is also used as our bathroom and toilet, and the old wooden door, after years of abuse and the work of wood lice, has developed a small hole by the bottom left hinge. As a bendy boy, I can squat and peep through it. Through the peephole I watch men revealing hidden curves and edges; the texture and shape of the ultimate taboo forms the contour lines inside my psyche.

And like all old buildings in Hong Kong, the wooden structure I had called home, a home where I learnt so much about myself, was eventually demolished in 1979, replaced with one of the characterless concrete buildings.

*

It is 2009. I am reading a love poem written for my partner to a roomful of guests, family, and friends from all over the world: England, Greece, Argentina, Hong Kong. It's my civil partnership ceremony in London—Westminster Town Hall, Marylebone, in the same room where Paul and Linda Mc-Cartney got married. I look up and see the happy faces of my brother and his wife, just flown in from Hong Kong. My parents have already passed away.

At the reception, a friend, a lay monk, blesses us using the same Orthodox wedding crown that my partner's mother used at her wedding in Athens. He pronounces us kings of our newly created family. He invites my brother to come out and crown us, holding the silk circles linked with a white ribbon above our heads. I remember the day he was brought to Aberdeen Street as a newborn baby. Faces of my family and neighbours come to me, most of them now gone. Disconnected fragments of my past fall into place, and shift like coloured crystals in a kaleidoscope creating a beautiful pattern—me. My eyes tingle; a tear brushes my cheek like a paint stroke. My partner holds my hand—I know, I am home again.

Intimate Strangers

By Germaine Trittle P. Leonin

W E first met in 1992, during our freshman year in the University of the Philippines College of Law. She was a bespectacled, serious-looking lady from Dumaguete, while I was a true-blue Manila girl who had lived in Quezon City for most of her life. She was quite timid and well tanned as any typical *girl from the provinces,* but was surprisingly articulate and fluent in English. Apparently, Cebuano was her first language, and her attempts at speaking Tagalog were often laughed at by people. They said her Filipino was "weird" because she would say "*aklat*" when referring to books instead of the more colloquial "*libro*"; and she would use the formal "*sapagkat*" instead of "*kasi*" to explain things and make connections. But early on, one could tell she was really smart, and with her degree in Political Science (*cum laude*, mind you), she was destined to become lawyer someday. I, on the other hand, had already paid my dues as an office girl in the Makati business district before I decided to enter law school as an afterthought. With my degree in Agribusiness Management, I had worked for a multinational for a whole year, and I was cocky and unprepared for the rigors of schoolwork all over again.

On our Orientation Day, we already had an assignment

and I stubbornly half-complied, believing I would not get called upon to recite out of two hundred freshmen. But as luck would have it, the professor, rumored to enjoy embarrassing students, called on me in an auditorium filled to the brim. I was pale and nervous, at the brink of fainting, but I decided to just wing it, for I had read the assignment, after all, albeit haphazardly. Out of all twenty issues cited in the subject case, I chose the main one, and fortunately, the correct one, to the utter disbelief of those who attempted to answer the same question. My friendly new classmate turned to me from her seat and congratulated me, for I had done well, she said, thinking on my feet like that. Years later, with our inevitable disillusionment with the study of law, I would remember what faith she had in my capabilities then.

Life in law school was hard and we welcomed support from whatever source, just to gain some advantage over our highly competitive classmates. That first semester, she joined the prestigious UP College of Law Portia Sorority, the only law school-based sorority in UP, and I followed suit the next semester. By our second year, law books and photocopied materials were fast draining our finances, and we both decided to become working or evening students. Working full time during the day did not leave much time for studying, and life as a law student was getting more difficult by the minute. Like many others, we were doomed to extend our stay in the college for longer than we would prefer.

After my father succumbed to Alzheimer's disease in 1994, I was forced to take a leave of absence from UP Law. I was socially out of circulation for many months, but she would come visit me at home since her office was very near our place. We also kept in touch even when she went home to Dumaguete during school breaks—on Christmas and in the summer. We were classmates, sorority sisters, and very good friends. But nothing could have prepared us for what was in store for us in 1995.

We had always enjoyed each other's company because of our common interest in books and reading. Being voracious readers, we would read almost anything besides our law books. We both liked watching movies, and we shared a strong affinity for animals, especially dogs. And while we both liked to write, she claimed that she was much better in non-fiction narratives, so I should just stick to my poetry.

Admittedly, she was mostly into Shakespeare, J.R.R. Tolkien, and Ray Bradbury, and I was into Stephen King, Erich Segal, and Richard Bach. While she was into opera and classical music, I was into popular rock 'n' roll. But soon, it did not matter; for we found ourselves learning to like each other's preferences, because we felt enriched by the other's tastes and experiences.

Strangely, in each other, we found the "walking encyclopedia" we were both searching for. If one wasn't familiar with a topic, all she had to do was ask the other who, more or less, would have some information about the subject. We could talk endlessly about anything and everything under the sun. When one spoke, there was always that spark of recognition in what the other was saying. We did not finish each other's sentences as a matter of practice, but we could always tell what the other was thinking.

We were once asked, "So, when did you stop being friends?" We replied that we never stopped. We still are each other's best friend. I cannot say exactly when, but somehow, somewhere, things did change for us and the connection became deeper than we could have ever imagined.

She once told me that she had only asked God to give her someone who was kind, patient, understanding, and loving. She had always assumed God would take care of the gender requirement, so maybe it was her fault for not being more specific. Meanwhile, my idea of a true soulmate was someone who would have the same values I had: God-fearing, family-oriented, generous, and caring. I had not realized that sometimes the one thing you're looking for is right in front of you, but you just don't see it at first.

I had always been aware of my same-sex attraction ever since I had adolescent crushes in my all-girls Catholic school. But while I resisted it, I knew I would have to come to terms with it sooner or later. It was much harder for her since she had always assumed she was straight, having had guy crushes before. I somehow felt guilty for "turning her gay." But as some say, "Weren't we all straight once, until we discover and accept we're apparently gay after all?"

We were unnervingly logical about the whole thing. We discussed it rationally and decided to resist whatever was developing between us because it was the sane thing to do. Imagine the friendship we could lose if things turned sour; we were sorority sisters, after all, and it might scandalize the residency and the alumnae alike. We thought that decision was by far the most difficult thing we could make. But after struggling with it for weeks, trying everything possible to avert a problematic situation, the decision to acknowledge our relationship for what it truly was, eventually became our saving grace.

We recognized from the very beginning the pain and the sacrifice that our love would entail. At the risk of being discriminated against and being fodder for the rumor mill, we just couldn't bring ourselves to deny our relationship and negate each other's value in our lives. That one act of courage cost us some people whom we thought were our friends.

Some sorority sisters shied away from us; others accosted us and intimidated us with questions, complete with religious morality lectures. Others merely speculated and whispered behind our backs. At the annual sorority ball, we became the highlight of the evening talk. Soon, the alumnae were hounding us, and I was so afraid they would make a move to expel us from the sorority. Eventually, the worst thing that could happen came to pass: after being a top contender for the highest position in our sorority, I was not voted Lady President during the elections.

At one time, during Holy Week, she got sick when she was all alone at her dormitory. I brought her home with me and took care of her. My mom and sisters had always liked her, and they suggested that she just board with us, so someone could always look after. For a while, they accepted her and tolerated our relationship. But things turned bad when my youngest sister got married and there were just too many complications. There was trouble about always having to explain my "friend's" status in the family. Our relationship did not get the same recognition and respect as my married sister's. Preference was always given to my brother-in-law, to the point that we were asked to give up our sleeping quarters for their sake. Eventually, a choice had to be made, and my family threw us out of the house.

We had nothing then but each other and the clothes on our backs. Using her savings, we rented a little rathole in the more distant and cheaper residential area of Project 8 in Quezon City, and scrimped and saved to be able to get the bare essentials of a home. We learned to scour downtown Manila, particularly the winding side streets of Divisoria, Quiapo, and even the Pier for the cheapest home furnishings. I, who had been accustomed to having maids take care of things for me, now had to learn to do household chores. I picked kitchen duty for I at least knew how to cook. Together, we learned to go to the wet market and pick out inexpensive foodstuffs. We were embarrassingly poor, but we had never been happier in our entire lives.

Once, she caught me sitting in our empty living room with my ear pressed against the wall. I explained to her that I was listening to the early evening news on the neighbor's television next door. She cried at that, for she knew what a TV-addict I was, and a TV was just not included in our priorities at the time. Meanwhile, I was always moved to pity when I would see her hand-washing all our laundry, when she had already developed an allergy to the cheap detergent we used. We couldn't even afford an iron then, so to avoid wrinkles, we used excessive amounts of fabric softener before hanging out our clothes to dry.

When our finances improved, we devised a way of purchasing housewares without being too conscious of it. We agreed that our gifts to each other would always be items on our priority list. So for a Valentine's gift, I gave her a washing machine. When she got a bonus, she finally got me a small television set. Later, I got her a new stove with my own bonus. And knowing how much I missed my tropical fishes back home, she got me a small aquarium for my birthday.

Although she was working full time then, I still had to get a stable, higher-paying job to help out. In those days, since I was still studying, we still had to scrimp to be able to afford tuition and school materials. She would buy me my law books and reviewers, and even give me extra pocket money when necessary. So when I graduated in 1999, I decided that the honor should be hers to come up on the stage with me as I took my Bachelor of Laws diploma. While the others brought with them their respective parents, or wives and husbands, she went up with me as my name was called. While our law professors looked on in confusion, my batchmates hooted their approval, and we just gave them naughty little smiles.

Presently, our life together is comfortable and familiar. We render mutual love, respect, and support; so who is to say that the love we share is any less intense than that experienced by heterosexual couples? We have closely approximated a married life as far as practicable, but in the eyes of the law, we are not spouses; we are mere strangers to each other.

We would like to get married, but the law says we cannot; that right is reserved by the Family Code for a male and a female alone. Although we have moved in together and have bought furniture, appliances, and other household items meant to be owned in common, these things we are enjoying jointly are not considered conjugal property. At best, under a presumption that it was taken from common funds, we possess them under the terms of co-ownership.

And since we are not spouses, we cannot be intestate heirs of each other; for only as a widow or widower can one be considered as a legal heir. So, to inherit from each other, we must each execute a last will and testament. In the same vein, under social security laws, we cannot be each other's primary beneficiary because we are not each other's legal spouse. Consequently, we cannot claim tax exemptions on each other for being married individuals.

Since we are not even considered next of kin, we cannot make medical decisions for each other, and neither are we authorized to make funeral arrangements for each other. The credit-card companies and the insurance industry likewise refuse to acknowledge our couplehood because we do not fall within their definition of "immediate family member."

And although relations with my family have significantly improved, sometimes we still experience this non-recognition of our partnership. When all the other brothers-in-law and sisters-in-law have been asked to become *ninongs* and *ninangs* of newborn nephews and nieces, my partner has never been asked to serve as a godmother. During weddings in our respective clans, when the traditional photo with the groom's or bride's family is to be taken, it becomes an awkward situation to explain since neither of us is officially classified as an in-law, and distant relatives or family friends sometimes ask.

Nonetheless, the people closest to us have tried to accommodate us somehow. My cousin endorsed her as her official wedding coordinator, when it was a position coveted by our other snooty cousins. Meanwhile, my partner's older brother asked me to be a reader for the mass during his own wedding.

Despite all these hardships, my partner and I have decided to spend the rest of our lives together and we have taken steps to affirm our committed relationship. In December 2000, we had our commitment ceremony by way of a Holy Union to show our families and friends that we mean for our couplehood to last for a long, long time.

On the eve of our Holy Union, she reminded me of an incident when we were still in UP Law. We were in the library with our classmates discussing the possibilities of ending up with one of our own batchmates later on in life. The guys were divided in their opinion of headstrong and intelligent women. She then asked one of them if he would consider marrying her. Typical male, he found it hard to commit to an answer and I blurted out: "I would… ," immediately chasing it with a qualifier, "if I were a guy, that is." Eight years later, she still remembered that rather weird experience.

In June 2002, we renewed our vows to each other. We had known each other then for about ten years, and we had been together as a couple for a total of seven years. On December 15, 2005, we celebrated our tenth year together. I have no regrets, and I hope neither has she. Truly, happiness is being married to your very best friend.

GIFT FROM GOD

By Alistair Yong

I USED to fear the long weekends because that is when the Darkness comes calling and I lose myself in it. Now that I'm back in my home state in East Malaysia, within the safety and sanctity of my parents' home, I can at least sleep peacefully. Yet, I can still hear the whisper of the Darkness, calling me again and again, clawing gently at the door of my soul.

"I am safe in this space," I tell myself.

After reading in disgust the news about two women being given six strokes of the cane in a courtroom in the state of Terengganu for attempting to have consensual sex with each other, I thought to myself that there are worse vices and more eligible individuals in Malaysia who should have been publicly caned than two women in love with one another. Such individuals include the eight men who brutally assaulted a transgender woman in Seremban; six of the individuals were only teens between sixteen and seventeen years old. What's more disturbing was that when police officers asked the men the reasons for their actions, they simply said that they just felt like doing it. Then there were also two portrait photos of LGBT activists that were taken down from a state-sponsored photography exhibition in Penang, held in conjunction with

Malaysia's sixty-one years of independence from British colonial rule in 1957. Yet these three incidents took place within a short period from May 9, 2018, when eligible Malaysians voted out an oppressive and corrupt government. The LGBT community thought we could finally breathe with relief, but alas, these incidents only confirm that the community has been and always will be an easy political target for discrimination in the name of religion and nation-building. What crap is this from hypocrites who blame the community for their own insecurities and shortcomings?

The gay community is often misrepresented, leading to misunderstandings about whom our community is made up of and what the community stands for. Since the most visible of us are perhaps the most outspoken and flamboyant of our community, we are labelled a sinful and hedonistic community. Our sin therefore is the promotion of an unhealthy and amoral "lifestyle" that has the potential to lead the younger generation astray. We must be kept in check or altogether eliminated, or so went the justification of a recent raid on a well-known gay club of more than three decades right in the heart of Kuala Lumpur. There are also those of us who prefer to lead quiet uneventful lives, small but valuable lives, like myself, retreating to the comfort of our own closets, weary of the onslaught of the outside world. Sometimes we share it with a life partner, but that is a rarity in this part of the world, a bonus in life, which I had the privilege to have. In my younger days, I belonged to the former group, a shallow member who frequented the clubs and saunas in Klang Valley. Ultimately I was looking for love, yet jaded by the shallowness of the scene,

I eventually believed that love in all its forms did not exist in the community, until Jonas unexpectedly arrived to prove otherwise.

My goddaughter Briana, an affable character with a big heart and an even bigger appetite for the finer things in life, has often chastised me for clinging to the past and not letting go. God bless her soul, for she has been the voice of reason ever since my breakup with Jonas. My argument for holding onto the past is that it gives value and context to the future; without the pain and grief that come with loving and living, there would be no perspective, no comparisons, no meaning. Naturally, I kept this to myself for I am never able to win an argument with her.

Jonas was only a year younger than I but more street-smart, way beyond my years. I met him in my early twenties. We dated, we had sex once in a while, and we parted. I did not see him for another few years. I was busy chasing guys not meant for me and getting my heart broken along the way. I believed that one must have their heart broken at least once or twice before one is done with love.

It wasn't until a few years after, when I frequented his salon for my monthly haircut, that we started meeting for dinners after he closed his shop. We shared the same problems and realised that we both went through the same cycles. Those days, recreational drugs were just taking root amongst the more affluent and highly sexed members of the community. This, I felt, was a pertinent issue that needed to be addressed sooner or later. We were both tired of the scene, since the people we met were never quite relationship material, and we wanted something more meaningful than the simple "touch and go." Somehow, things just fell into place for both of us, and we left our promiscuous lives. We both strengthened our resolve to fight this and build better lives together. We met for breakfasts over the weekends, sometimes he stayed over, and we gradually developed an integrated routine together. We decided to move into a rented room in 2012 and lived frugally, satisfied with the love we discovered for each other.

Thus our relationship began with baby steps. It was with Jonas that I understood the meaning of learning to love someone. There were no explosions of love, no butterfly feelings; it was just an affinity for one another that came naturally, as did the idea that maybe, just maybe, we could have a relationship together. I hesitated at first, but my confidante and confessor, Noel, told me to enjoy it while it lasted, to "just be in the present." Yet as more mornings went by as I awoke beside him, my heart whispered to me that I could do this forever, I could be married to Jonas. I had read about such love in novels but only then had I the chance to experience it.

And it was during this period of love that I made an inner vow that would one day haunt me: I loved Jonas so much that I told myself, should we break up, I would bear the greater burden of the pain, for I could not allow Jonas to bear the greater pain. When I shared this with Noel, he reprimanded me, "Always in the future huh! Never in the present. You just started a relationship and now you are already thinking about the breakup!" I got a slap on the head. Little did I expect, this would be a self-fulfilling prophecy, and I wasn't as strong as I thought I was.

There were nights where I had bad dreams; Jonas would hold me down, his hands on my chest. His frame smaller than mine, but sturdier, he would prevent me from falling off the bed as I thrashed and screamed in my nightmare.

"You had another bad dream," Jonas would say.

We would get up and laugh about it before holding each other for a moment, and then turning to our respective sides of the bed and dozing off. I thought, if we could laugh together *at* each other, there must be some love and understanding between us. He was my rock, and much like how he held me down in life, he kept me grounded to prevent me from being swept away by my lofty ideals and passions like a stray kite in a storm. I felt that there was something good coming, something that would last a lifetime. The next morning, we would have breakfast at our usual stall in a hawker centre in Sri Rampai before going to work. The stall owner would eventually ask if we were brothers since he thought we looked similiar, and we would exchange cheeky expressions. During Jonas's working weekends, I would sometimes prepare lunch for him and deliver it to his salon. His colleagues would tease him by announcing in Cantonese, "Your cousin-brother has arrived."

I still recall that our last Valentine's Day dinner was in 2016, at Franco's Restaurant at Avenue K. Jonas and I watched a Chinese movie, *Mermaid*, at KLCC. I thought the film was rather badly done, but who cares when you are in a steady relationship coming into its fourth year? Time and time again, Jonas proved himself to me, even during the times I was back in my home state of Kota Kinabalu for a few months. The day after the dinner, he posted photos of us having dinner on his Facebook page. I depended on Jonas for specific things, things like upon hearing a song in Mandarin, I would ask him what the title was. To this day, I have yet to find a song by a Taiwanese singer that contains the lyrics, "Meet me at the church," or was it, "Kiss me in the church"? Such things remind us of the casual vacancies of the roles that once were in a relationship. How then can we simply let go of things when we are never quite the same after a relationship? Simple rituals such as using a hair dryer, when during my single life it was a nonexistent item in the bathroom. I still use his pair of Nikes for my gym shoes because they just fit so comfortably, like no other shoes could.

During our Valentine dinner, I also realised I had to do the ordering for Jonas, as the menu was all in English. I resigned to the fact that it would be me taking the lead when it comes to ordering at Western restaurants whilst he takes the lead during our visits to Chinese restaurants. Could I ask for more, or should I have asked for more, but who can have a partner who is both faithful and loyal, and this was something I valued more than anything else. Would I date someone of my type (during my younger days) at the expense of the two values I mentioned? No. I don't even know what my type is after Jonas.

I used to think that meeting a hot man in a crowd and dancing with him, or someone who took my breath away, or someone who suddenly took a genuine interest in me, were magical things. I was gravely mistaken because I discovered that simply sitting next to someone you love, reading with him whilst both your toes touch, getting up early together or watching the other sleep in silence, or using the same bathroom in the nude, these were also magical acts of mundane love. My fond memories are mainly of the nights when we retired to our bed; he would be catching *The Voice of China* on his tablet, whilst I would be watching *Once Upon a Time* on my notebook, before we kissed each other good night.

In this relationship, I learnt that despite not being able to choose who our partners are, for they truly arrive unexpectedly, like gifts from God, we can choose to love our partners. We grow together despite our differences, we assist in each other's growth, sometimes even in cathartic growth, and it is only when one journeys together with the significant other can the relationship truly grow. I didn't know then, but there was something about Jonas that told me we'd grow old with each other. We promised each other that we would make a trip to Japan during winter to see snow together; we never did make it. Yet my error would be revealed to me soon enough. One night in the third year of our relationship, he came home from a long day at work and I wasn't sober—I hadn't been for a few days in a row. He got so mad that he broke the door of our room. That was the first time I witnessed his rage at me, and I burst into tears. He saw me collapse and rushed to cradle me while we wept together, "Why? Why do you do this to yourself?" That was when I knew he truly loved me, but it was too late, because it also marked the beginning of our breakup. When men weep together, we see the divine in the other, for where tears fall it is sacred ground.

The last time I felt his eyes gazing over me and his bodily

warmth was after a short threesome in a seedy hotel, painful in my heart, yet he allowed me to stay and, exhausted after two nights of not sleeping, I lay beside him with my head on his left hand. He always had a special scent distinct to my nose, and I could see his new tattoo. Someone who loves you will be able to see you in your ugliest form and yet still love you all the same. Once upon a time Jonas loved me as such.

"Rest and I will wake you up later," he said without looking at me, his right hand busy messaging on his phone.

That was the last time I felt the closeness. He lifted his left hand and my head collapsed to his torso, his hand resting on my torso and gently stroking me to sleep. I must have ground my teeth, but I was too immersed in what I knew would be my last intimacy with Jonas. Not a day passes without me thinking of him, and praying that he is happy. I wonder if he still thinks of me. I wished that we still talked, and then I asked myself, isn't that the hidden desire of my cunning heart trying to lead me back to a false hope?

With Jonas I tasted infinity, which is why I found the breakup so painful and challenging to overcome. I still keep a picture of him by my writing desk; in it, he is happy during our Valentine's Day dinner at Franco's. He smiles at me here with his distinct almond-shaped, hazel-coloured eyes as if to remind me of our failed relationship that beckons to be witnessed in all its inadequacies and its beauty.

When we first dated he had only a single tattoo on his left arm, to which he gradually added through our relationship. Now his Maori print tattoos are fully extended on the left side of his body and arm, right down to his forearm. He had strong hands developed from long hours at the salon making his clients beautiful. I was never quite attracted to a person with tattoos but with Jonas, I began to be accustomed to them, even to admire them, though it never crossed my mind to get one myself.

One night when we were not staying together anymore, he called to ask if he could stay for the night as he had just completed the last portion of his tattoo, a seven-hour session. He was too exhausted to drive back home. When Jonas arrived at my doorstep, I saw the dried blood flaking from his back and some parts were still oozing with fresh blood. He asked me to wipe it and rub his body with moisturiser.

I listened while he told me that he already had two relationships since we broke up, whilst I secretly wished that somehow the past would be made right: "I wish I paid more attention than take things for granted with you, I wish I didn't say those horrible words to you, I wish I had better self-control, I wish we still talked and that I can say that my heart still aches for you." However, the past can never be made right. It can only be remembered and honoured, thereby giving more context and depth to the present and value to the approaching future. So there I was, the ex, the mid-thirties dreamer who had no ambition. He confirmed that we couldn't be together anymore as I was living in the past and that he needed someone stronger.

"I need someone who can cover me," he said, "not drag me down in life." The words left unsaid weighed heavily upon my heart. "Better for one of us to survive and be successful in life than the both of us to perish because of love," he concluded.

I listened whilst each word was like a knife being driven slowly into my ribcage towards my heart. Not a word was said after that as he eventually settled back on his side of the bed. Sometimes, it is easier to live within the comfort of one's own delusions. By the time I finished attending to his flaking skin, he was already snoring. I switched off the light and pulled a thin blanket over his naked torso. I curled up beside him and stole whatever intimacy I could.

Through the night, his tattoo imprinted on the bedsheet; even until now, I am reluctant to use that sheet as with each wash, the tattoo gets lighter, much like how I fear the memory of our relationship will fade away into oblivion. There are nights where I lie awake and imagine he is still sleeping soundly beside me, but he is not there anymore. He belongs to someone else, or someone else shares his bed. The hardest part for me was getting used to sleeping alone after sleeping next to someone for almost four years. I remember at the start of our breakup, he informed me through WhatsApp that he would be moving out the minute he finds a new place. His reason then was that our objectives were no longer aligned, that I wasn't ambitious enough. The reasons for our actions are never due to a single reason, but a culmination of reasons.

During the post breakup period, I developed a prurience towards my ex and his new intimate relationships. Subconsciously I was also trying to re-create our intimacies with my new intimate relationships, which resulted in more damage for my mental health and spirit. In order to escape, I resorted to a dangerous vice to numb my pain, one that I thought I could control. Studies have shown that hookup apps provide some momentary relief from anxiety and depression, especially if there is good sex. Add recreational drugs to it and you will have potential mayhem and a truly vicious cycle. If the issue of gay men being more likely to suffer from poorer mental health isn't bad enough, the issue of recreational drug use will prove to be an even bigger problem for the community.

Thus began the destructive cycles into the Darkness, brief at first and for longer periods as time progressed. I fed the Darkness that grew within me, making each battle with substance abuse more difficult than the previous one. Does anyone know the battle that takes place within oneself? Except for God as my witness, with each walk into the Darkness I spiralled further and further into desolation whilst my support systems began to disintegrate one by one; my circle of friends and then my pillar of faith began to crack. My performance at work began to suffer and finally I was left with my final refuge: home. I decided one night to leave the city for good, whilst looking over the balcony with the vibrant view of Kuala Lumpur and contemplating the journey down from the thirtieth floor of the condominium. I was so close to the edge but the fail-safe switch of my Catholic upbringing was strong enough to pull me back from it. When we are close to the edge, we sometimes wonder if we were ever in control. My memory weakens, I feel it disintegrating with my walks into the Darkness.

At the breaking points of my struggle, I WhatsApped Jonas for help and support. During the initial months, he came, but gradually he stopped coming, and that really drove the point home. What hurt me the most was, how could you not care for someone you used to love, someone whom you shared a bed with for the previous four years. If it were Jonas, I would still drop everything and rush to his aid. Yet I know that that is a poor comparison. It is the comparison of a romantic, hopeless fool.

These were days that I truly missed Jonas till my chest ached, and I daresay he made the right decision to leave me when I could not control myself any longer. Now that all hope has ended with the declaration that he is with someone, I have to halt all efforts in attempting to resurrect an already-dead relationship. What still burns alive is the love in my heart. The love that persistently asks the question, "Could it still be possible?" but perhaps the Christian notion of love within me and its expectations are very different to a person who is not exposed to it.

It is heartaching when one is banished into the past and has no part in another's future, especially if that person is still so very dear to us. We constantly reconstruct the past and future in relation to an alternate present. The present becomes a sort of prison. With every path and every corner, every vehicle that passes by or individual that crosses my path, there is a glimmer of hope that it will lead me back to Jonas. Such was my prison for a period of time. Perhaps this is what the term "living in the past" means. Torment teaches us what the heart has forgotten.

This Darkness, this evil that still courses through my veins as it silently courses through the community, is a social ill. It silently plagues the gay community, creating depression and hopelessness amongst members of the recreational drugs circuit. Yet what could I do? Perhaps simply bearing witness to it, to simply take account of what is really happening is enough, I thought as I began writing about it. Writers are bearers of truth and to be a bearer of truth is to suffer truths more deeply than others. Half struggling, half sober, half weeping, I tried to find my love for the writing craft again. Will it save me?

Despite the realisation that Jonas has left, deep down I still truly have a place for him in my heart. He came to me when I didn't believe that love and relationships could ever exist for a gay man. He came to me when I didn't believe in love anymore. He left me when I started believing in it again and when I had to begin walking on my own again, and for that I am forever indebted to Jonas, for despite me repeating that I wanted to grow old with him, the problem was that I didn't listen; he didn't want to grow old with a person like me. I looked up the meaning of his name. Jonas in Hebrew means "Gift from God." What God giveth God taketh back, and I've lost what I've lost, so I must struggle to keep what I still have. So help me God, I prayed silently to myself and for Jonas. What is the point of praying for someone who doesn't feel for us anymore? Especially for someone who is already absent from our lives. I continued to ask myself, can we stop loving someone after a breakup? I got the answer gradually during the period of my recovery, that if we truly loved a person, we don't stop loving him, and we just learn to be at peace with that love from where we are.

We found our way to Heaven together, but along the way we both got lost in Hell and had to find our own way out. I got lost in the Darkness and took a much longer time to find the exit. All this is the past, and though I am unable to let go of it, I have learnt to live with it. At the very least, my heart is now able to wonder about the possibility of a third relationship. My mind warns me that this might be the last, which leads me to naming this possibility as my "No. 3," who has yet to arrive. However, I whisper to my heart that I am just too broken for another relationship, that I would not be able to mend myself again should I shatter into a million little pieces in the Darkness.

For now, please be still and silent, my beating heart, allow me this moment to reminisce about my sweet Gift from God, Jonas.

A Common Language

By Hayley Katzen

MID-morning, April. I stroll beside a river in Sha-tin, a semi-residential area in Hong Kong. As I pass the silent swings and slides of a park, a see-saw of foreign words pipes through speakers where women practice tai chi, their figures cast like chess pieces along the pathways. A slight woman rotates a large pink plastic wheel, and when she looks up, our eyes meet for a moment. After the solitariness of the country roads and paddocks of my Austra-lian life, I feel a quiet joy here amidst these other morning exercisers; I'm alone and accompanied.

Eight months later in the early hours of the morning at an Australian New Year's Eve dance party, I clasp my girlfriend's hand waltz-like and press up against her as we move with the rhythm. When she wearies of the wordless doof-doof music and the writhing sweaty bodies, she heads for the hay bales outside. Now I dance alone. I toss my head back and feel the wig's long purple hair trail down my back. I close my eyes, breathing in the dance party music. It starts under the soles of my knee-high leather boots, cours-es up my thighs in their sheer black stockings, beneath the black velvet minidress clinging to my torso.

Beyond the Shatin park in the shaded corridor outside the red brick Marriage Registry, I watch a group of twenty women dance a routine of steps. Some wear track pants, some tights or trousers. Some move mechanically, others add in their own wiggles. At the front a woman in a diaphanous black blouse scans a page crowded with Chinese characters, selects a song from her iPod, and then leads the dancers. A voice curls out from a portable speaker. My body stands mute, not answering this unfamiliar rhythm.

I merge with the dance party beat. I am the marionette; my shoulders and arms, my pelvis and hips, my legs and toes twitch to the puppet-master's saxophone and drum beat. I lift the purple wig to cool my wet neck, feel the damp between my breasts and thighs. Gyrate, pulsate, shimmy, shake, stamp, stomp, thrust, twist. I lose myself in the rainbow of swirls that pulse up on the screen. I revel in the pageant of feather and leather, gowns and micro-minis, headdresses and harnesses. Here too I'm alone and accompanied: no need to speak or interact. I smile—even as I move position when the scent of amyl nitrate pricks my nose.

A woman in a shirt studded with diamantes invites me to join the group. In the back row I take one two three steps left then right, then a quarter turn. Repeat. When I find myself in the front row I giggle; I don't know which foot goes where. Between songs I chew on the offered dried mango and ask— with key words and comic gestures—if the group are rehearsing for a performance. My host translates; the others titter.

Eventually I understand: they dance for exercise before going for yum cha. Our communication exhausted, I step back and we all smile.

A woman with a naked stomach and skimpy shorts dances up close to me. She mirrors my movements; she's everywhere I look. What to do? Has this woman misinterpreted my movement? Is she coming on to me? Or is she just friendly? If I dance back, might she think I'm interested in her? I'm uncomfortable with the language of the dance floor. I pray she'll leave me alone, pray my girlfriend will return. My limbs lose the rhythm; I squeeze shut my eyes.

When the women walk off the cement outside the Shatin Marriage Registry I presume the class is over until someone hands me two fans. With a flick and a flourish of the fans an extra panel of blue fabric cascades and weeps. I do it again, and again, and then notice the women taking their places. I join the back row, mirroring their movements and suddenly in my thick-soled runners and shapeless shorts I am graceful and soft and flowing. Now the voice from the speakers snake-charms my body. Now, alongside women whose names I don't know, where our common language is dance, where there's no innuendo or expectation, where the fans are my only partner, I sway and step.

A tap on my shoulder. I open my eyes to a silver-haired friend wearing a black fedora and cranberry lipstick. She hands me a black fan emblazoned with golden moons and stars and blazing fires. I seize on it as partner and prop, fling it open and fan my friend and the strangers around me—the sweat-wet men, even the woman with the naked belly. I fan my head to my heart and I am again inside the rhythmic beat. Twist, twirl, sway. Again I speak a language that is communal, that needs no individual response. Again my heart soars amongst bodies whose names I needn't know.

CROWS LIKE US

By Edward Gunawan

O NCE, there was a crow who admired the beautiful singing voices and the elegance of the sparrows.
Longing to be like them, the crow left his own
family to live with them.

*

A man leapt to his death from the twenty-fourth floor of a
hotel in 2003. Last seen in good spirits by a hotel employee,
he ordered a glass of orange juice on the balcony outside of
the hotel's gym. His friend, who was waiting to meet him in
the lobby on the ground floor, heard a commotion and rushed
outside. She later identified the man as Leslie Cheung.

*

Just a few years ago, I started drawing a triangle on my wrist
during the darkest hours of my last breakdown.

With a black marker, I traced a straight line parallel to my
veins. Then I continued it across at an angle, before connecting it back up to the top of the first line. One by one, over and

over again, I drew the lines—down, across, and up—until the little diagram was completely filled in.

I imagined myself as a robot, pressing this pause button to stop the thousand paper cuts of thoughts and emotions whirling and swirling inside me. *All will be well, all will be calm.* A break, a breath, before I pushed on this button a little longer. A reset, a re-start. *Poof! I'm a new character in a video game.* I imagined what I'd come back as in my next life.

I did this to pass the time. I did this to distract myself. I did this so I did not have to choose between noodle soup and chicken rice for lunch.

Before I knew it, it was already 5pm and I was still in bed, still wearing the same clothes I went to sleep in the night before. Another day, another night. Another bed to be made, another plate to be washed, teeth to be brushed, and laundry to be folded. They blended and blurred together. Everything became a chore. All felt pointless, endless. All I wanted to do was stop.

*

The crow learned to sing and fly like his new family. For a while, he was happy. But he could never shake off how different he was from the sparrows. His feathers were black and as much as he tried, he croaked instead of sang. He questioned his place amongst them.

*

Leslie Cheung was one of Hong Kong's brightest superstars, whose music and film career spanned over three decades.

Heralded as the "King of Canto-Pop" by the Hong Kong media, he released thirty solo albums and had a fan base that spread beyond his homeland and the Chinese-speaking diaspora in Asia and North America, to South Korea, Japan, and Europe. An accomplished songwriter and an electrifying performer, he broke records with his live concerts, which are still considered the gold standard of excellence in the region.

Leslie was also an award-winning actor who starred in over fifty films—many of them box-office hits. He received international acclaim with his moving portrayals in films such as *Farewell My Concubine* and *Happy Together*. CNN referred to him as one of "Asia's 25 Greatest Actors of All Time."

Leslie was charming and stylish, dubbed by fans and the media as the "most beautiful man from Hong Kong cinema." He was successful and beloved. Tens of thousands of mourning fans in face masks attended his funeral procession, braving the SARS epidemic that was at its peak and had kept most of Hong Kong citizens indoors.

His suicide note began with the word "Depression!"

*

I remember the first time I wanted to stop. I was about ten years old.

I had been sent to Singapore for school, away from my family who were still living in Jakarta. A male stranger molested me in the changing room of a shopping mall. The abuse catalyzed the affirmation of my same-sex attraction and further complicated my sexual discovery—a process that would have been rife with confusion and fear to begin with for any child.

A few years earlier, when I was six years old, I had stared at a poster in a laser-disc rental store for a minute too long. I was searching for a cartoon I had not watched yet when I looked up and noticed the shirtless soldier posing above me. A dog tag nestled snugly in between his glistening hairy pecs. I reminded myself, "But I'm a boy."

Dad encouraged me to play sports, an activity I never enjoyed. Even my older sister, who has always been very athletic, did not throw balls "like a girl."

After catching me playing with my cousin's Barbie dolls, Mom asked me in a taunting tone, "Do you want to be like them?" I knew even then not to reply affirmatively. Besides, as much as I loved brushing that blonde synthetic hair, sweeping it up into a glamorous bun before letting it cascade down freely, I had no intention of becoming a professional like the hairdressers and shampoo boys in our neighborhood salon.

But that derision in her voice stayed with me. The same tone used by her friends—animated and chatty housewives who appreciated getting their hair cut and washed by these deliciously bitchy, mostly effeminate men. The gaggle of them would erupt in laughter after sharing a joke, but as soon as the "girls" were out of earshot:

"Arik just broke up with his *friend*. That's why he is so mopey," one neighbor said, offering her insight. "Yah lah, what does he expect? People like them will come to no good end," another one would chime in. In *that* tone.

I knew then not to be like them. I knew not to *want* to be like them.

I know now that it was not the molestation but the unexpected ensuing arousal that led me to re-enact a scene from the local soap opera, swallowing a strip of aspirin one night after the changing-room incident. *I don't want to come to no good end*, I must have thought. Only a few years later would I learn: not all pills are the same.

*

The crow returned to his own family in the hope of finding a place to belong. He was welcomed back, but soon his crow family realized he no longer croaked nor flew like them. He was ostracized and banished from his own home.

*

Born in Hong Kong in 1956, Leslie lived abroad twice.

The first time, he went to school in England as a teenager. A year later, he returned home and shortly made his debut in the entertainment industry. After achieving early fame—fitting in the public idea of a charismatic heterosexual heartthrob—he moved out of the country for the second time, migrating to Canada with his long-term same-sex partner Daffy Tong in 1990.

Restless and disconnected, Leslie emerged from his early retirement after a few years in Vancouver and returned to

Hong Kong once again. This would become the most ground-breaking and successful period of his career.

He received international recognition for his portrayal of an androgynous Peking Opera star for the film *Farewell My Concubine*, which was awarded the Palme d'Or, the highest honor at the Cannes Film Festival. He went on to star in *Happy Together*, directed by legendary director Wong Kar Wai, which is now considered a gay cinema classic.

He also explored and reflected his gender-bending sexuality through his music. He released his theme song "I" ("我") that opened with the lyrics "I am what I am," echoing the seminal queer self-empowerment power ballad from the musical *La Cage aux Folles*. He directed his own music video that showcased a homosexual relationship through dance–movement performance art. In his 1997 *Passion Tour* concert, he shocked and delighted his audience by pairing his clearly visible masculine stubble and muscular build with feminizing waist-length hair and tight skirts. Several news outlets reported he also danced seductively with a male performer in a pair of glittering crimson high heels. Those "red heels" have now become a defining symbol for his queer sensibility.

Emboldened, he publicly announced his long-term relationship with Daffy Tong during the concert. Even though he would still self-identify as bisexual and he did not personally consider this a "coming out," Leslie became one of Asia's first gay icons.

In the more socially conservative era of post-AIDS hysteria, when gays still faced stigmatization and marginalization, Leslie's defiance sparked controversy but his popularity surprisingly did not dim. His star appeared to shine brighter than ever.

Behind the scenes, however, Leslie was unraveling.

*

The second time I wanted to stop, I was twenty-one years old.

I have been driving for the past couple of hours. I don't know where I am going and why or how I have gotten onto this freeway. One moment, I am saying goodbye to my best friend after a late-night coffee, and suddenly I am on Interstate 5, somewhere between Los Angeles and Bakersfield.

The speedometer climbs from 110 to 120 miles per hour. With only my two headlights cutting through the darkest night, I cannot make out what is ahead.

The past year had been a turbulent one. Leslie committed suicide and I was outed by my ex-boyfriend's parents. I could have offered *It was just a phase* or *We were just experimenting* as deflections. Intent to break free from the constant lying imposed by my closet, I saw a chance for me to bridge the growing disconnect between my parents and me. I allowed them to finally know who I really was. Am.

I remembered the first time I read about Leslie's coming-out a few years before. It was the first time I saw someone who looked like me—Chinese—and was brazenly out. I also saw the couple—Leslie and Daffy—who appeared to be affectionate and loving to each other in the media, as a much-needed positive representation of same-sex partnership that countered what would be considered a "degenerate lifestyle" in the region. There was hope yet.

When news of Leslie's death broke, Mom commented in passing, "See, that's what happens to people like them."

As my foot presses harder on the gas pedal, I remember the birthday card Mom sent me for my twenty-first birthday a few days earlier. Accompanying it was a letter in which she shared about a documentary she had watched. A reformed gay man had "successfully" married a woman. Mom wrote, "See, it's possible. You can be cured. You too can be happy."

I had been trying hard to be that happy in that way, for their sake and mine. My parents had consulted with a psychologist in Indonesia who touted the success of "conversion therapy." To please them, I obliged and went along for a series of hormone tests and therapy sessions.

Perhaps I thought my parents would come around after I underwent these. That they would come to see there was nothing wrong with me. Most likely, I was also curious. A part of me wanted to be "cured." I wanted to have a better life. An easier one. A happier one. A life without what I would later learn to be "minority stress." This was something my parents would be familiar with. They lived through two major upheavals in Indonesia in 1965 and 1998, when Chinese Indonesian minorities were raped and massacred. I understood that's where my parents' love and protection came from, and I desperately sought shelter in it.

There is not much of a barrier between the road and the 150-foot mountain cliff. Should I continue, I will drive myself off to a crashing blaze. That wouldn't be so bad, I think. It would be a respite to stop it all. My head is spinning round and round, each

thought faster than the one that came before, faster than my speed-
ing car. I can barely keep up.

Ang Lee's *The Wedding Banquet* began playing in my mind. I had watched the film with Mom when I was a teenager. The movie centered on a gay Taiwanese-American man who married a woman to appease his parents. The movie's happy ending, in which the parents came to some acceptance of their son's gay identity, was plausible only in America, it seemed to me then. Mom drove this point home: "There are no gays in Asia. They are only in the West." For her, gay was a Western phenomenon, despite the hairdressers she encountered almost every week. Or her son. For her, the gays—*they*—were there. And there were no *them* here.

Yet there I was in the West, having come out in America, expecting that there would a ready-made community waiting to embrace me, after the rejection from my own parents. I found myself even more isolated from the LGBTI community.

Around that same time, while grieving over the death of an ex-boyfriend who had died from a drug overdose, I waded through the sea of men as I began to date and diet in equal fervor, desperately trying to fit into the narrow stereotype of what an "acceptable" gay man should be. Many other gay men of all races and ethnicities have experienced body-image dysmorphia or social marginalization. As a racial minority in the U.S., especially in the pre-dominantly white gay culture, these feelings were further accentuated for me. I came to learn, like Leslie perhaps did, that Sparrow-land may not be a place for this Crow.

I can hear the lyrics to a Peggy Lee song, "Is that all there is?" before the car comes to a screeching halt right at the edge of the cliff. Yes, there has got to be something more than this.

*

In the later part of his career, thinly veiled accounts of Leslie's depression became public knowledge. His partner would later share that he had attempted suicide the year before his passing.

In several news reports, Leslie's family said a chemical imbalance led to his depression. But being one of the first and highest-profile gay icons in Hong Kong, that made him an easy target. Perhaps that contributed to his mental fragility too. In several local tabloids, Leslie was frequently vilified as a "transvestite" and described as "perverted" or "haunted by a female ghost." His Passion Tour concert, while acclaimed in Japan, Korea, and Canada for his daring, almost defiant display of queerness, met with disapproval and condemnation in Hong Kong. In several newspaper accounts, he confided that he planned to retire from stage performance completely because of the depression caused by the disparaging comments about his gender-crossing concert performances. The music video he directed (that featured the same-sex performance art dance) was banned from the biggest TV station in Hong Kong as well. Author Nigel Collett would later theorize that Leslie's depression may have stemmed from his struggle to come out completely as a gay man to the public.

Whatever the cause of his depression might have been,

Leslie became a cautionary tale, shouldering all of the burden as the most visible queer representation in the Chinese-speaking world. Perhaps Leslie too had the same thought as I did: like AIDS, depression was a malady gays had to accept as our fate. That a tragic end is the only inevitable conclusion befitting crows like us—alone or dead.

Perhaps.

*

The third and final time I wanted to stop, I was thirty-three years old.

I am all alone in bed in my Bangkok apartment when I begin to draw the triangle on my wrist. As I trace each line, I remember returning to Indonesia just a few years earlier, attempting to find some solace and meaning back in the land of crows. Even though my family and good friends know about my sexuality and I am already out as a gay actor back in Los Angeles, I regrettably shoved myself back into the closet when I embarked on my own film acting career in my home country.

I convinced myself to follow my talent manager's advice not to frequent the gay clubs in Indonesia. "People just need to know me as an actor. Not a gay one," I told my close friends when they invited me to join them for a fun Friday night at the local hotspot. *Let someone else do it. There are other gay actors in the industry*, I rationalized. *They are further along than I am. Their career probably won't take a hit. Who am I, this newbie nobody, to make an impact anyway? I'm no role model. I'm not an activist. I just want to act, damn it!* Perhaps thinking, if I said it enough times I could absolve myself from the responsibility.

Ironically, the first movie part I landed was in a very gay film. I played the only straight male role in a film of all gay male lead characters in the sequel of *Arisan!*, one of the first Indonesian movies with a gay theme. The director was a progressive pioneer who frequently tackled taboo topics like polygamy, women's issues, gender, and sexuality. The conditions were conducive for me to come out. But Leslie Cheung, I was not.

I remembered the many successful out Asian-American actors during my time in Los Angeles. I was cast in Alec Mapa's show, where I learned how irreverently witty and completely himself he is. Alec would later adopt a child with his long-time partner. On the cover of *The Advocate* magazine (a leading LGBTQ monthly publication in the U.S.), there was BD Wong, a successful stage and TV actor, with his newborn twins. But perhaps Mom was right. Alec, and BD may look like crows but they really are sparrows.

I escaped to Bangkok as my acting career wound down. I did not get to be the actor I wanted to be, nor possess the courage that Leslie had. I felt I wasn't getting the opportunities that I expected; I felt passed over for roles. An actress friend advised me to "butch it up." A casting director friend privately confessed that the negative PR that would result if the public learned about my sexual identity made him uneasy to cast me in any of his projects.

What I do suspect, though, is that I was also not a very good actor. Stifled by the closet I had imprisoned myself in— feeling like I had to constantly watch myself even when there was no one looking, I was living one big performance then, layering one mask onto another. *How was I to play another character when I didn't even know how to play myself?*

I had already experimented with a behind-the-scenes career as a writer, director, and producer by then. When the opportunity to produce a feature film in Bangkok came up, I took it. I completed two films and reveled in their success. But as hard as I worked, I was partying even harder.

Dancing under the giant disco lights with a circuit party-full of shirtless Asian gay men in a haze of chemically induced euphoria, I remembered the relief and guilt for leaving my gay friends back in Indonesia who married unsuspecting women due to social pressure and in some cases, family inheritances. Acquaintances suddenly disappeared after the loud whispers through the grapevine of their struggles with AIDS. Their families did not even hold funerals.

I remembered the look of despair in a young man's eyes who offered, "Why even bother coming out? It won't change anything anyway."

My friends and I took turns propping up one another's sweaty bodies as we fell into drugged stupors in the middle of the dance floor. We could hook up with anyone we wanted. We could get drunk and take all the drugs we desired. We slept till we had to work. We worked so we could party all night again. We were having the times of our lives. *This is freedom, isn't it?*

I had followed in the footsteps of close friends who not-so-jokingly swore to life-long bachelorhoods in anticipation of countless breakups and heartbreaks. Jaded and emotionally impenetrable, we sought solace and meaning in our career advancement, material accumulation, and online hook-ups.

Then there was the numbing dark hole that these self-medications had carved into me. They only made things worse. As I tuned out all of the despair and loneliness, I also obliterated any fun or joy I had left, until I could no longer feel anything anymore. No color, no texture, no sound, no smell, and no taste. Everything had turned black—black as the sea at night and I was drowning in it.

What the hell is wrong with me? I thought then. *Other people have real problems. I was successful. I have everything I could ask for. So why don't I feel like I'm winning? Why do I feel like losing to this dark hole, this black sea?*

Leslie's oldest sister had shared in an *Oriental Daily* interview that Leslie himself had often wondered, "I have money and so many people love me. Why am I depressed?"

I have beaten this depression thing before! I thought. This was the part I did not get.

"See, that's what happens to people like them," comes the familiar refrain from Mom. *What she meant was crows like Leslie and me—birds of a feather, perched on that intersection of sexuality, race, and nationality. Crows stuck in no-bird's land.*

There is nowhere else to run to. There is no exit, no escape, no country left for me to move to.

Again, I hear Peggy Lee crooning, "Is that all there is?"

Instead of drawing the triangle with a black marker, I imagine replacing it with a kitchen knife instead. Pain will be something, and anything will be better than nothing at all.

This third time will be the charm. I will succeed so I will not have to feel like a failure anymore.

*

Mental health-related suicides disproportionately affect us in the LGBTI community.

Many reports reveal that there is a high correlation between being a sexual minority and experiencing mental health challenges such as depression. As such, many of us in the LGBTI community are more prone to contemplating and committing suicide than the general population.

This high rate of depression and other mental-health issues has been attributed to "minority stress"—the discrimination, marginalization, and stigmatization that LGBTQs experience. We respond to stressors more adversely—stressors that our heterosexual cis-gendered counterparts also face— job losses, breakups, and grief over lost loved ones. Even if we have come out, we still experience "trauma of the closet," which has been likened to the effect of PTSD. Perhaps due to double-minority status, racial minorities in the West and women are at even higher risk.

Where there is support, however, there is a reduction in suicides. There have been many advances to alleviate the social stressors, especially in the West. The increasing quantity and quality of LGBTQ portrayals in Western media has changed social attitudes. But in Asia, while social conditions have generally improved, formal anti-discrimination laws and policies to protect sexual minorities are still lagging. In Indonesia, there has been the witch-hunt humiliation of the gay sauna raids in Jakarta and public canings in Aceh. In China, portrayals of LGBTQ characters are banned in the media. Even in one of the most liberally progressive places in Asia, where same-sex marriage was approved by its court, research co-sponsored by the Gender/Sexuality Rights Association of Taiwan reported that almost 20 percent of Taiwanese gays and lesbians have reported attempted suicide—a 50 percent higher rate than the general population.

Correlation, however, does not equate to causation. Being LGBTI is not a precursor to suicide. This is worth repeating as it was not initially obvious to me and, I suspect, many others. I grew up hearing and reading so many tragic news reports for so long that they have become so deeply ingrained in me. I had believed that a sorry end is the only conclusion for people living with depression and other mental-health challenges. The dearth of stories about individuals who have contemplated suicide but succeeded in thriving, as well as overly reported sensational celebrity suicides due to mental health challenges, further perpetuates the negatively skewed narrative that depression leads to suicide.

In fact, I had internalized and lived with shame and minority stress for so long that I equated being gay with depression and mental-health issues, and thus suicide. I thought I deserved this tragic end. I thought this was the only way.

Perhaps this was what Ellen Loo was also thinking. In 2018, fifteen years after Leslie's death, the lesbian singer-songwriter from Hong Kong was reported to have committed suicide after her long struggles with depression and bipolar disorder. She had just publicly come out with her wife the year before.

*

It was a long time before I realized that the story of the crow did not need to end as in the book of Chay Yew's plays where I had discovered this fable. I can continue it to change the ending.

This crow would meet other crows like himself—birds who had defected from both families. Birds who were neither crows nor sparrows, but both crows and sparrows. This bird would also meet other displaced sparrows too, like my partner Jake—an American who has lived many years in Asia. We may be a ragtag flight of misfit birds flying and sounding a little funny, but we can still sing. We can soar.

*

I remember Leslie fondly, as many of us do.

I admire him for his light and his presence. I miss his courage. I am still inspired by his ground-breaking work and the comfort and joy it gave me. I miss him very much.

But Leslie lives on. Fifteen years on, Leslie continues to attract new fans who have only recently discovered his work and was voted the third "Most Iconic Global Musician of All Time" (after Michael Jackson and the Beatles) in a 2010 CNN poll. Every year, many of Leslie's fans still gather outside the hotel where he took his own life to commemorate his passing. Some become visibly emotional talking about and remembering him.

I often find myself wondering how Leslie would be if he were still amongst us. Would he stay as charming, as handsome? Probably. Would he still be producing great work now? Most definitely. How would his wedding to his partner look? Would they even have one? Would they have children? How many? What other ground-breaking work would he share with us now? How much more joy, how much love would he give to himself and others through them?

We will never know.

*

The sky appeared bluer, framed against the red rocks of Sedona, Arizona. Jake joined my parents and me for a road trip in 2018. It was the first time my partner joined in a family holiday. A grin escaped me as I watched Jake taking photos of my mother posing with the requisite Asian double peace-sign gesture.

This moment is the accumulation of those difficult times in my life. If I had not come out fifteen years ago, if I had not continued to press play through all of those times, this moment would not have come.

*

I am not immune to depression. I know that there will be many more times ahead when I will encounter it again.

That's when I will come back to the triangular diagram on my arm. I will draw each line, one by one, over and over again. I will do this to pass the time. I will do this to distract myself. I will do this to press play—to keep on, carry on, live on.

I will remind myself that: as pointless and hopeless my life may feel at that moment, I know that this dark hole, this black sea, is not all there is. Only by continuing on does this crow get to write a different ending.

L FOR LATITUDE

By Ingvild Solvang

THE *waria*-queen swaggered and swayed on unsteady heels, flaunted her black hair, breasts, and golden glitter, forcing her mouth around lyrics in a language she didn't speak. Bravery—that night and every night—is beautiful, and we loved her. It was November 2000 in Kaliurang, Central Java. Underneath our feet, Mount Merapi was bottling up volcanic pressure. Four hundred HIV/AIDS activists, members of Yogyakarta's LGBT community, and allies that gathered that night were unaware of the pending eruption. Two years earlier, Indonesia had shed Soeharto's regime. Caution may have replaced the initial post-dictatorial euphoric sense of promise, and some already spoke with nostalgia about the former authoritarian regime, but *reformasi* stood in people's hearts and minds when the queen raised her fist in the air for a grand finale. Her act was quickly followed by a poet, who spoke to a strong political canon about love and acceptance with melodramatic voice and gestures, but when his face froze in a grotesque grimace, and he gasped and locked his eyes on the back of the room, I thought it was a performance until bangs and then screams began rolling from behind.

I had arrived in Indonesia from Norway as a student of

social anthropology a few months earlier. I had welcomed the idea of a year in a predominantly Muslim society believing naively it would help consolidate my identity, make it more whole somehow. In my twenties, I lived a proud, at times militant activist life inside a Norwegian gay movement that was on a winning streak. In the space of a few years, I had gone from being a lonely teenager achingly in love on an Arctic island to starring with a girlfriend and my mom in a documentary on national TV intended to break barriers for gay rights. Soaring oil prices were turning Norway into The Richest Country in The World; gays and lesbians were appointed as government ministers; and my love life turned wonderfully heartbreaking and chaotic. And with so much to celebrate, I was the brat who felt that the queer claimed too much of my identity. I had a need to balance it out with something un-queer, like Indonesia. Equipped with ill-informed stereotypes about Asians and Muslims—Muslim women in particular—living subdued by conservative culture and social control, I thought it possible to travel and escape myself.

Barely a week in, Intan proved me wrong. She spoke to me from the side of the street as I walked by. She was sweetly butch; she laughed loudly; she drank beer and worked in a bar where she hoped to catch a break and reach something different from what her mother had dreamed for her. Meeting her so soon showed me how new tracks were paved with past experiences. I met lesbians and gays, and the *waria*s, which literally translates to lady-men. I soon discovered they belonged in my new world alongside mosques, traditional village structures, and cultural norms blind to their existence. They were a paradox, and with the untrained eye of a newcomer, I at first understood their world to be akin to my familiar, European liberal normal. Intan and I embarked on a relationship, and we were soon caught off-guard by the rugged terrain across cultural, but also social, and economic differences. While often fun and wonderful, we trampled on each other's boundaries with incompatible definitions of "love," "friendship," and "trust." I was in a state of profound culture shock that felt prolonged and intensified by Javanese social norms that discourage open confrontation and "loss of face" around my cultural ignorance. I would see nothing but smiles until patterns behind my back suddenly drew my attention to my miscommunication and unacceptable behaviors.

Homophobia also suddenly appeared. Once I had seen it, I grew paranoid. Someone wrote "lesbian" in the dust of my window, and I wondered whether the black scorpion on my living room floor could have been placed there. Intan did her best to guide me around her culture, but she also often left me lost. But that night in Kaliurang, as I clung to the back of her motorbike up the slopes of the volcano, we shared the understanding that attending an HIV/AIDS awareness event wasn't a particularly good idea given a rise of politicized Islam, which motivated young men into action against "immorality."

Bravely or foolishly—depending on the narrative I chose—we suppressed our inner voice of caution and went regardless, Intan and I, together with two other friends: Tita from East Java, and Mie from Belgium. We watched the performance from the floor in front of the stage. Behind us, rows of chairs had filled up, people standing along the sides.

Everyone was watching the poet's face, deciphering his grimace, reading it, registering that his expression wasn't a part
of the performance, that something had yanked him out of
his poem, and that we were watching his transformation from
confident to frightened. Rapidly repeating blasts as if from
machine guns were heard when chairs crashed to the ground
as the crowd leapt forward toward us, fleeing from something
unknown and roaring at the back of the room. My instincts
lifted me off the ground. I ran, while Intan chose to dive onto
the floor thinking she would rather be trampled than shot.
While my leg muscles flexed, Intan counted *satu–dua–tiga* for
the number of people that bounced, ran, and toppled over and
on top of her. Person number six stepped on her head and
broke her front tooth. I was the second person, who bruised
her back. It was only the first horrible thing I did to her before
our ordeal was over.

Fear sharpens the senses. Time slows down. The air thick-
ens. I moved as if through water, sounds distorted as if trapped
at the bottom of an aquarium. My thoughts came in complete
sentences. For the first time in my privileged life, I was sure
about facing death. "I may not get out of here alive." "Why
am I running?" I repeated the question to both everyone and
no one around me, trying to make sense of the danger before
me that I still hadn't seen. I squeezed my way through a side
door, only to meet a crowd retreating from the other direction,
and in the maelstrom of bodies, I was shoved to the front line
where I first saw one of them, a man. He wore a scarf to cover his face. He was picking up unopened Coca-Cola bottles
from a red crate to hurl at us. His eyes were dark and angry.

Allahu Akbar. A hundred men maybe, with sticks, masks, and machetes shared the chant.

Someone behind me held me like a human shield. I could only lift my arms to protect my face. When I turned my head, I saw blood streaming from a man's neck from being hit by a smashed bottle. A *waria* crouched beside me. Mascara left traces down her cheeks; she panted, frantically pulling at her short skirt, wishing for it to cover more of her muscular thighs to hide the gender battle that made her the most visible and vulnerable of us. The aggressor looked directly at me. He shouted and smashed a bottle to the floor by his own feet creating a black pool around him. "Why waste ammunition?" I thought and realized in that moment that he wanted to scare me, not kill me. I wasn't the most vulnerable in the room. Different levels of "us" and "them" emerged in my understanding of the situation. I was there with the LGBT community—our "us"—but as a light-skinned European I was visibly an outsider to our attackers. It was his fellow Javanese in the audience that fueled his rage and disgust the most. I placed an arm around the *waria* to my side. And I told her we were going to be okay, but what I actually meant was, "I will be okay." Enough space had been created amidst my fear to think about fighting back. Had we come prepared for more than music, love, and compassion that night, we could have outnumbered them. I knew that for now they had the upper hand, but my Norwegian lore told me that action would be taken, and justice, eventually, would surely be served.

When every bottle, chair, and surface had been smashed, they left as soon as they had appeared. Shaken and damaged, we found strangers, friends, and lovers to hug and whisper words of comfort and encouragement to. I found Intan. She was covering her bleeding mouth with her hand, but beneath stampeding feet she had heroically grabbed Mie's lost camera bag. Together she stayed behind with Mie, who had the instinct to photograph the damage. Meanwhile, Tita and I went outside to start the job of untangling our motorbikes from a pile with smashed headlights and slashed saddles.

The story didn't end there: the mob came back a second time, Tita and I ran for the darkness of the forest. Now separated from Intan and Mie, the two of us sat in the undergrowth from where we could see silhouettes of raised sticks and hear more shattering windows, screams, and *Allahu Akbar*. They were not done yet. People were crawling and crouching in the vegetation around us, and we didn't know whether they were with us or them, except the conspicuous *waria*s, who had stripped out of their dresses hoping to save themselves while squatting naked between the shrubs. Tita turned her palms up and launched her prayer to her own Allah, pleading to get home safely. I saw irony in these different versions of the same god.

Tapping into my newfound awareness as a foreigner, the "outsider," I pulled Tita along through the darkness, away from other people in hiding. I gambled that making it to a road while pretending we had nothing to do with the event, the LGBT community, and who we were, we would be safe. We walked through the forest for no more than a kilometer before we hit a road and a small street stall under the yellow light of a kerosene lantern. It was a surreal alternate universe where we sat down along wooden benches among strangers. We ordered hot teas to blend in. We tried to act nonchalant and not terrified, leaves and twigs in our hair, striking up a conversation: "Does anyone know where that noise is coming from?" Anyone around us could have been an aggressor. When our tea turned cold, we were left without options but to ask the food stall owner to bring us both back to the venue on his motorbike. We made him stop at a safe distance from where we could assess the situation. By then the police had arrived at the scene. Dressed in civilian clothes, they were guarding the entrance. I demanded—with the entitlement of a Norwegian citizen—that they identify themselves. They sternly brushed me aside. There were no signs of Intan or Mie, so we returned alone from the mountain on Tita's bike. On the way we passed the police barrier, and saw dozens of men in scarves held back by the side of the road. We drove on looking straight ahead.

We reunited with Intan and Mie at Mie's house, where the four of us spent three days together, holed up. We were startled at the sounds of motorbikes. We slept in one room, afraid of being alone. We each had a different story from different vantage points from where we had taken cover. We shared each and every detail of what we had seen, heard, and thought. And Intan and I began to diverge. She had her tooth fixed. She could smile again. I insisted on more radical healing. Mie and I, both Europeans, attended a meeting by local NGOs to denounce violence. Intan thought it was pointless and went back to work. I was outraged that she didn't appear to fight. I couldn't fathom that injustice would prevail. I asked questions about the attackers, where they came from, how they were funded, what they believe in. Intan shrugged. It was what it was.

Just a day after the NGO meeting, all attending organizations withdrew from the initiative. Highlighting opposition to a minority that was holding the majority hostage with such violence was too risky.

We found out that the detained men had been released without consequence. A newspaper quoted the police expressing their support of the aggressor's agenda: "The sex party had to be stopped." At very least, the police expressed their concerns for the methods used by the vigilante group.

I learned what Intan already knew: that the system wasn't there to protect us. Having always had a Norwegian trust in state institutions, this first-ever feeling of such disempowerment changed me profoundly. For the first time I understood how vindictiveness and violence live inside me too. I realized that a very Norwegian self-righteous sense of being "a good person" stems from the trust that the State will channel our ugliest emotions into justice and fairness. In this absence of justice, unlike Intan, I didn't come equipped with the spiritual strength and patience required to reinstate inner peace and balance of my external behavior for the sake of communal harmony. These mechanisms instilled in the individual and the community, the remarkable ability to find balance between an uncertain future and a violent past, were lost on me. Instead, the injustice that I felt on my own skin made me desire running wild, taking revenge, hunting them down, smoking them out. I dreamed about a fierce counterstrike. I used evocative, violent language when describing what I had experienced, and how I believed we should all respond. I got furious with Intan for being so *pasrah*, so fatalistic, and able to take it, absorb, incorporate the experience into her flesh and bones. The silence that met my rage made me turn on her. I didn't recognize that it was the bigots' hatred that kept detonating along the gaps of culture, history, and experience between us. At the same time and in contrast, the shared experience of trauma brought Mie and me, two fellow Europeans with similar emotional and political interpretations of the attack, closer together. And, doubtless from Intan's perspective as an extended rupture of violence, Mie and I fell in love. And, finally, with my betrayal, Intan responded with grief nearing madness. She cut my eyes out of photos and hid skull-and-crossbones-labeled bottles around my house. It wasn't entirely undeserved.

Blinded by my own emotions, with a Western sense that I mattered so totally as an individual, I failed to see that to Intan our attackers might have been her neighbors, old school friends, and brothers, not just a faceless political fraction of a foreign country. She must have learned with absolute certainty that by asking for the right to love me and for me to love her in peace, she was asking too much. I couldn't comprehend the cost of her resistance.

*

This attack on the community didn't have the power to alter Indonesia. In my life, however ironically, the violence locked me onto a new trajectory. Nearly twenty years later, Mie and I sometimes joke that our—now—marriage is built on post-traumatic stress. We walked through our stages of trauma in sync: the initial fear followed by anger. About six months after the attack, on a Saturday afternoon, we were overcome by a need to *know*. Exploiting our disguise as foreigners, we played ignorant tourists to infiltrate an Islamist street party. Moving away from victimhood, we sought empowerment from more knowledge about them. We needed to verify the known stereotype that these men are a mindless "mob for hire" without any true ideology. Similar groups of young men are observed as large motorcycle gangs obstructing traffic, expressing a hysteric masculinity through uniforms, screams, and fists in the air, while they carry flags of various political parties and Islamic groups. That particular Saturday, we watched them. They enjoyed friendships and tea in the shade, while being entertained by sexy *dangdut* dancers. Most of them seemed more interested in having their photos taken with us than discussing ideology. Somewhere in an old album are the photos of us posing with smiling men in uniforms and Mujahedin-labeled T-shirts. Among them were those who shared their belief that gays, communists, and Jews are an immediate danger to society and country.

I wasn't in love with Indonesia after my first year there. I had lost myself between geographical, political, and personal latitudes. Returning to Norway, I felt relief. Still there was Mie, and she was still in Indonesia. I might have thought about closure when I boarded the plane again another year later. This time, however, Indonesia sucked me in with that magic so many foreigners experience. It's difficult to explain to Norwegians, who enjoy such wealth, and stability, that with uncertainty comes a creative energy and vibrant force that makes me feel more alive. My one-year adventure slowly turned into nearly two decades. I have now lived nearly half my life in Indonesia. My life is patched between these cultures and countries. A transnational life means freedom from cultural expectations, but also rootlessness, not really belonging anywhere.

Mie and I got legally married on my Arctic island in 2010 with my family as witnesses. My nieces performed a dance routine to Britney Spears's "Womanizer" at the party, and the neighbors raised the flag to celebrate our love as they would any other, showing that Norway has kept making strides toward the mainstream acceptance of LGBTQI rights. Bringing our life script back and forth between continents, Mie and I made the decision to have children one night while drinking Tiger Beers at a street café in Timor-Leste.

We read up on the ways for two women to have children. The Norwegian state dictates that artificial insemination at a nationally recognized health institution would grant my partner automatic status as co-mother provided we were married before conception. However, with our lives firmly established in Indonesia, we chose a friend as donor, who had also been with us in the attack. We had gotten to know him well over the years. We shyly asked him, and he took our proposition with him on a silent meditation retreat. He came back with a heightened awareness that he had a purpose to make people happy. We calculated my ovulation cycle and met on my most fertile day. With the help of a needleless syringe, I was pregnant immediately.

Our arrangements provided the father not only with a child but also a partial solution to the dilemma of gays in Indonesia: the pressure from relatives to start a family. We had created a win-win, and other friends hailed the event as historic: "No one else has ever done this in Indonesia before!" they claimed. One dear Javanese friend gave us a complete *Mitoni* ceremony as a gift. The Javanese ritual performed at seven months of pregnancy is created to ensure a safe birth for the mother and child, and a good future for the family. Before the event, the *dukun*, an elderly woman renowned for her spiritual services to the royal court, came to our house to discuss the event. She enthusiastically embarked on the challenge to translate the script to suit a foreign, lesbian, expecting couple. It had never been done before, she assured us. In front of seventy invited guests, most of whom were dressed in traditional Javanese outfits, she had me wear a cape of jasmine flowers over a *kebaya* while kneeling to kiss my wife's knee in gratitude that she would take care of me and the baby. Seven selected guests showered me in water from seven different wells. Our neighbors were tasked with representing my Norwegian family, and they safely captured the two coconuts—a male and a female—which I symbolically gave birth to. The *dukun* prophesied the birth would go well. My wife and I served *dawet* drinks, which guests paid for with ceramic money, symbolizing our commitment to working together for the family. Any alterations to the Javanese worldview served more than anything to show that as an expecting couple—lesbian or not, foreigners or not—our aspirations didn't differ all that much from others.

We gave birth to our daughter at a natural birth clinic in Bali, choosing a place where our family in all its facets was welcomed and celebrated. The birth itself was the most profound immersion in universal humanity we will ever experience. The Hindu midwives broke into song when the baby arrived. Appropriate procedures for the placenta were ensured to prevent misuse of its potent spiritual powers. When our daughter was three days old, the midwives and a visiting Japanese friend piled onto our bed and together we used candles to burn off the umbilical cords while I sang a melancholic Northern Norwegian *vise* and held the baby tight. Our Jewish bungalow neighbors broke bread and blessed our baby on the Friday entering her first Sabbath. Before she was three months old, she had also been prayed for by Muslims and blessed by the clerical representative of the Norwegian Seamen's Church in Asia. Having a child brought a new sense of place in the cosmos. It solidified my feeling of belonging in multiple places. My child was transnational in flesh and blood, heart and soul. We raised her to speak four languages surrounded by loving people of all creeds. We planted her placenta underneath our mango tree on Java. Some of the soil we sent off to the Arctic oceans from a Norwegian beach, and in Belgium, some of it went beneath a rose bush in the garden of our Brussels home. We've since had a second child following the same recipe. All the while, Norwegian, and Belgian bureaucracy has struggled with how to deal with our family from a legal perspective. Having trodden a new path of transnational and alternative family, bureaucrats and computers in each country don't know how to process our version of love. Securing rights for children, mothers, and father has been a Kafkaesque quest.

Being queer parents also places us in a new category of LGBTQI activists. It is no longer about us, but about our children. How can we support their healthy development, which relies on their positive perceptions of us as a family? Before the kids, I could flag or tone down my queer identity at will and pick my battles. With children, I continuously have to decide how to respond to situations like a taxi driver's questions about my husband: where he is, whether he is Indonesian (which he obviously must be, given my girls' tanned skin). I've been adamant that the girls know the truth about how they came into being, and they started asking questions about it already around the age of two. This also means the girls will know when I lie to strangers to protect them from potential ignorant and harmful reactions. My elder daughter was about three years old when I first noticed her choosing her own path of least resistance when meeting new people: "I don't have a father." This response in conservative societies generates another set of inquiries, which again will influence the narrative she crafts about herself. As a mother, I want to protect my children; however, as a queer mother anywhere, and particularly in conservative societies, it is necessary to postpone the hardest battles for when the children are ready to fight for themselves.

Every day my children walk into a potentially hostile world, and we cannot always be with them. In choosing schools, academic quality and tolerance become equally important. We have no other option than to be open about our family constellation from the outset. Our children will happily share their stories about their two moms, and we need schools with teachers who will embrace that. Our status as foreigners shields our family from much local judgment. We enjoy support and rarely face rejection, a risk so strong for local LGBT friends that it might deter them from coming out, not to mention considering having children. We may catch ourselves feeling paranoid when our child is not invited to a birthday party, or a child declines our invitation. However, reflecting on my life in Indonesia, I believe that I experienced blatant homophobia—like the writing on my window in 2000—mostly during the time I shared with Intan, a local girl. I was collateral damage when they came for her.

An Indonesian lesbian friend, who lives a secret double life hidden from her family, told me that our actions as foreigners are irrelevant to the improvement of her situation. We may provide local people with positive opportunities to meet a gay person and a same-sex family, however there is not much we can say or do as foreigners to sway local public opinion. On the contrary, our voices may trigger common claims that LGBT rights are based on values imposed by imperialistic, neo-colonial Western powers.

A part of our "otherness" is also knowledge that when Indonesia becomes difficult, in the ebbs and flows of politicized, conservative sentiments, we have the means and the freedom to leave. For many members of the Indonesian LGBT community, this is not an option. And the point is that Indonesia is their home, the country they love, and where they want to be.

*

When a backlash hit the Indonesian LGBT community in 2016, the LGBT issue flashed into the spotlight of mainstream discourse. Before 2016, the LGBT community sometimes came under attack by militant groups during specific events similar to the one we experienced in 2000. However at a personal level, LGBT people could largely fly under the radar and generally get away with "don't ask, don't tell" at home and at work. The *warias*, who are visibly non-conforming, have always been vulnerable to ridicule, harassment, and sometimes also physical assault. However nothing compared to the unprecedented surge of vitriol and violence against LGBT persons in 2016. Full-blown moral panic and paranoia hit common Indonesian communities. The term "LGBT" became a household word synonymous with "evil," "sick," and "dangerous." The sentiments were triggered and fueled by anti-LGBT statements by government ministers, officials, religious clerics, and medical professionals.

As an example of the fear-mongering, the Minister of Defense compared the LGBT movement to a proxy war, one more dangerous than the threat of nuclear warfare. And, while the president remained silent for months, the militant Islamist movements needed no further encouragement to capitalize on this sudden tailwind. The city of Yogyakarta, our home for so many years and a city previously known for its tolerance, was soon decorated with anti-LGBT banners. On almost every street corner, the public was informed that gays are mentally ill, pedophiles, perverted, child molesters.

The aim was to create an image that LGBT people are everywhere, ready to destroy religious faith, community, and family. Most dangerously, dehumanizing of the LGBT community: comparing us to animals and illness; blaming us for tsunamis and earthquakes; making us legitimate targets for legislators, law enforcement, and the ignorant public. Every day I passed the propaganda on my motorbike while bringing my children to school. I observed how once again, the system and the majority were unable to stand up for the most vulnerable members of the community. Instead, many doubled down on ignorance and hatred. It triggered fear and sadness on behalf of Indonesian friends, and the country I had grown to love, which had so generously given me a life rich with experience. While trying to appear brave, I quietly prepared our passports in case we needed to leave as the militants again threatened violence, and realized I still hold onto so much shame: after twenty-five years of work for the freedom to love, bigotry still has the power to fill me with terror.

This time, differently from in 2000, I wanted my voice to be deliberate and thoughtful, balanced against the outcry of my Indonesian friends: the *warias* who were forced into hiding; the young, closeted lesbian we know, whose girlfriend broke up with her out of fear; our friends with PhDs who saw the lost battles accumulate into a lost war. On the day that militants staged an anti-LGBT rally through Yogyakarta, and while the bravest among my friends marched against them, I went for a run through the city to observe from a distance. I was there, but this time, I was sadly stripped of the naïve belief that the good is destined to prevail, given enough

time. Fighting back is necessary, and Indonesians are in the
front line. In a globalized world, the homo- and transphobic
outcry in Indonesia is a response to the victory for same-sex
marriage that I benefit from in my country. The previously
silent Indonesian majority has found a need to assert its "Indonesian Values." This included some of the people we knew,
whom we had assumed were allies. I hit a deadlock in 2016.
Regardless of what someone says about their god loving everyone, my family and I still represent their worst fear: the
legalized, alternative family destined—they believe—to cause
the breakdown of society and eternal condemnation of those
"lured into the LGBT web." When I look at my family and
the life I have created, it makes no sense.

Mie and I stayed in the background of meetings, diversity
trainings, and events for courageous people to tell their truths.
I discovered how the hatred from the outside made the love
and unity on the inside stronger, and I now felt so much a part
of this "us." I remembered so vividly that night in Kaliurang,
before the terrorists entered, how we sat so closely together on
the floor in anticipation of the show to start. I looked at happy
faces all around, and I held Intan's hand. I knew then that I'd
done so much right in my life for having reached that exact
location that night: surrounded by beautiful strangers, a new
language, and a rich culture that made me feel loved. Taking
care of each other is the most powerful act of resistance.

The year 2016 became that line in the sand for us. On my
own, I could have compromised. But our elder girl had started
to read. We couldn't accept that her road to school was littered
by anti-gay propaganda. We couldn't let our children grow

up in a system that condemned their existence. At the same time, bigots should never be allowed to claim victory. Making a move from Indonesia meant leaping into new adventures, new countries, and possibilities: a decision which was inevitable for us at some point, regardless.

In 2017, we moved to South Korea, not exactly a liberal haven. My wife has not obtained a spousal visa from the Korean immigration, and I have faced predominantly Christian protestors at Seoul Pride, but we've found our way. We have chosen a school in Seoul, which without ambiguity commits to standing beside our children, and for "Rainbow Day" a teacher asked to borrow our rainbow flag, which she hung by my daughter's classroom.

As the kids grow older, they start to show an interest in love and relationships. The girls come home from school and taunt and tease about falling in love with someone of the same sex, calling it "so gay," and we talk to them about love being love. We know they are still too young to take on this agenda they had no choice but to be born into. It is challenging for them to be insider–outsiders everywhere they go, as biracial, multilingual, and transnational kids. But we're giving them latitude in preparation for that day when heroines are called on to make a difference.

Note: Some names have been changed.

DOES YOUR NAME MAKE YOU GAY?

By Huang Haisu

A T seventeen, I moved from home into a college dorm room with nine other girls who, like me, were learning a degree in English. Since then, my birth name Haisu seemed not to be good enough, so I began the hunt for an ideal English name that was right for me. I used many until one stuck. But that wasn't the end of finding myself. I continued to look for myself in the men I was dating. I watched them, heard them, smelled them, kissed them, had sex with them, until one day I felt totally at home, sitting across from a new friend—the woman I married. My search for identity made it clear that the English name that had stuck with me for years needed to go.

Harbin, China

At our campus on Kang An Road, English major freshmen were ready for the program orientation. I sat among my roommates, whom I had just met. We were excited to be meeting our teachers.

Our dean spoke to us for the first time: "Many foreign teachers have difficulty pronouncing your Chinese names.

Don't ever lose the chance to communicate with them because you don't have an English name."

"Do your best by creating your own English-speaking environment," continued the dean. Her voice was unquestionably firm. Her words became my mantra.

Claiming the best English names propelled us into a promising term. Before the first day of class, my classmates and I buzzed around dictionaries like forager bees, in search of suitable foreign monikers.

And like bees, we harvested names like Apple, Cherry, and Melon. We then graduated from flora to fauna, calling ourselves Panda, Monkey, and Zebra, and even adopted the names of predators like Tiger, Dragon, and Lion. Others eschewed the natural world in favor of Happy, Lucky, and Melody.

I preferred names that I had personally encountered, like the fictional twins Lucy and Lily in my seventh-grade English textbook. I was Lucy in the spring semester, then Lily for the fall. During the break after the first year, I watched a soap opera on TV in which a female lead, a short-haired professional woman, had a reputation for getting things done. Her name was Chris—a perfect name for my following sophomore year.

That year, I met my American literature teacher, one of the few foreign teachers our dean managed to hire for us. A retired Taiwanese American (whose name I have forgotten) from the state of Mississippi taught us to read with the assistance of highlighters, conveniently boxed for sale to students. Along with the highlighters were free DVDs about Jesus.

All was fine, except "Teacher America"—named for being

the only teacher from America—had a problem with my new name. She called, "Chris!", I answered, and that was it, the end of my dream of being my TV idol Chris. Teacher America paused, pondered for a moment, and then spoke to the whole class.

"*Listen.*" She whispered, as though she were sharing a secret with us.

"Homosexuals—" (Upon hearing the word "sex," we blushed) "—would be what we in America think of as a boy with a girl's name, or a girl with a boy's name." Teacher America scribbled on her attendance sheet, then announced four more letters to be added to Chris: T-I-N-A. My sexually perplexing future was fixed. I was officially a straight girl.

Confusion ensued. I definitely was confused: what was so bad about being gay, especially in the supposedly free United States? Nonetheless, Chris had officially morphed into Christina, bringing the pressure of pronouncing a three-syllable name. Each time I introduced myself, I felt a cramp clutch my tongue.

Near the end of our first sophomore semester, Teacher America told us she would not return in spring. News of her departure came as a total surprise, as she had always expressed how much she enjoyed teaching us. She was like everyone's grandma, generous of spirit with a pinch of stubbornness to boot. Whether her departure had anything to do with her distributing Jesus DVDs in the classroom, no one knew.

Teacher America was forever gone, but in her honor, I spent countless hours practicing tongue-twisters to help me say my "gay-proof" name properly. It was as though she had

tied a knot in my brain, making me forget my original goal—
to try different names until I selected the best one for me.

Hong Kong

Ten years after my name change, I met my writing classmates
and faculty on our Kowloon campus. We were studying to
earn our MFAs in creative writing. As one of the few mainland Chinese in a program taught by award-winning writers,
I entered a portal that encouraged intensive self-examination.

During my two years of study, I wrote obsessively about
a character whose experiences were similar to mine. I was
trying to understand myself by writing about those whom
I loved, both men and women, for various lengths of time.
Teacher America would be disappointed to learn that the
gay-proof name bestowed upon me had failed to do its job. I
began questioning why I would continue to use a name that
did not serve its purpose. By the end of my writing program,
I was signing emails with my birth name, Haisu.

Abandoning my alias was difficult, for I could neither ignore my past nor the people who knew me as Christina. My
dean's message from 1999 played nonstop in my head: "Don't
lose the chance to communicate because you don't have an
English name!" After Hong Kong, as I met more people, I
self-pollinated English and Chinese names, introducing myself as Christina for employment and Haisu for the simple
pleasure of hearing my given name spoken by others.

But my names have cross-pollinated: people at work became friends, and friends found me new jobs. I forget who
knows me as Christina and who knows me as Haisu. What

a mess.

Knoxville, Tennessee

Early in the morning after the 2018 New Year, I was donning my goggles at the YMCA pool when I heard a man's voice ask, "Are you Chinese?"

I looked up. Through my already-foggy goggles, I could see a Caucasian man in the water. He seemed delighted when I answered "Yes." In Chinese, he introduced himself as Tian An, then switched to English: "It means *grace*," saying "grace" as though it were a password for an undercover mission. Since my password for the pool was "swim," we didn't seem to be on the same mission.

Grace was gone by the time I got out of the water, but he left a gift for me at the lifeguard stand. I unwrapped a brown plastic bag to discover a DVD about Jesus. Déjà vu, I thought. Eighteen years ago, I received the same DVD from Teacher America. I had an epiphany—I would no longer introduce myself as Christina.

My Name Is Haisu

At the age of thirty-five, I am grateful for remembering and connecting my experiences in three different parts of the world. I feel I have solved a jigsaw puzzle of myself. Transforming into full Haisu required living openly and honestly. During my transition, I was surrounded by hot water like a silkworm in its cocoon, leaving soft, shining silk for harvesting. Although frightened at times, I have lived as who I am and received the ultimate reward: "a sea of silk," the meaning of my name Haisu.

FROM BEAVIS (M)
TO BEATRICE (F)

By Beatrice Wong

FROM childhood, I hated seeing myself with short hair, T-shirts, and trousers, or my dreaded boys' school uniform. I never brushed my hair. I never chose my own clothes or eyeglasses; I felt annoyed when I went shopping with my mom and she would ask if I liked what she picked for me. I wasn't being rebellious. I was riddled with self-hatred. I felt so ugly when I was wearing T-shirts and trousers or my school uniform. When I went out in those shitty clothes, I would look at the floor all the time, and people would worry that I had self-esteem issues. Before I was ten, I would only look up when I saw girls wearing pretty dresses. The dresses were magnetic, they were the things that made my world spin. I really LOVED dresses, I had a folder full of magazine and newspaper cuttings of dresses, and I really wanted to touch a dress. Unfortunately, my mom was pretty tomboyish, so she only wore jeans. She only had one dress for special occasions, and she would never let me out of her sight because I was too small. So I turned to the alternative—other people's dresses. I lived in a crowded part of Hong Kong, and it was statistically impossible to not bump into another body. It's also criminally innocent when a little kid with a stupid face and oversized eyeglasses, who appears to have low self-esteem and doesn't look up when walking, crashes into a woman and this kid's hand brushes against her dress and sometimes her thigh. Yes, that was me. Did I ever feel bad? No. There was no sex education about consent or Twitter hashtags back then. Casually sexually harassing women on the street became second nature, but I knew that wasn't the endpoint.

And then I turned ten, which to my mom was old enough to be left alone at home while she went grocery shopping. This was the first big break in my transgender career. Putting on her dress was blissful, the first time I had ever admired myself in the mirror. I didn't care that I looked like someone's grandma. I really liked the feeling when the smooth, silky dress lining brushed my body. My underpants were in the way, so I removed them and immediately felt a sharp tingle in my nerves. I "peed" (nobody talked to me about orgasms back then) and was hooked. Conveniently, my desk was located in my mom's bedroom due to my dad's crazy interior design skills, so I "peed" whenever I could, even when my mom was just cooking in the kitchen a few feet away. I felt fine doing this because there wasn't any sex education about atypical sexual desires. Until... I got caught in the act. I had mistimed my mom's cooking endeavors. There was dead silence when I ashamedly changed my clothes and hung her dress back in the closet. It appeared she too wasn't educated in atypical gender behaviors, so at first there were no words in our dictionaries to speak about what had happened.

My mom finally found the appropriate words: "Son, were

you just curious about what wearing dresses felt like?"

"Yes, Mom, I won't do it again."

She went back to cooking, I went back to doing homework. That was the first time I felt I had done something wrong, and I never touched my mom's clothes again.

But I looked for substitutes. Like wrapping a towel tightly around my legs, tank top undershirts pulled down below my waist. Mom would always complain about the yellow "sweat stains" that never went away, and about having to buy new towels and undershirts. I played dumb and this went on for years. When I was around fifteen, we moved houses. I finally had my own room and pocket money too. I set about buying a dress; for months I hesitated, I made plans, and I went to a stall at the Ladies Market with zero customers. It was supposed to be a simple transaction: I would point to a dress and hand over the money, and the stall keeper would give me the dress. Period. But no. I would have to indicate the size.

"Er…"

"Are you buying for your girlfriend? What is her size?"

My heart rate went up to 200 BPM. I had been in a boys' school my whole life. There was no girlfriend, not even a girl friend.

"Are you still buying?"

"Er… she's about my size."

"She's muscular?"

And finally, the transaction and the full stop I longed for.

I learned about thrift stores afterward. They're a paradise, but at the same time, they're a paradise like Las Vegas. The odds may not be in your favor. There might not be a dress in

the right price or size or feel, and you leave empty-handed.
Most importantly, though, there is no need for human interaction. Still, I had prepared responses in case the occasion
arose.

It's for a drama.

It's for a school project.

My classmates at that time were obsessed with porn and
girls, and would brag about possessing a magazine or a tape,
or having dated a girl. One classmate decided to become a
pioneer by organizing a porn screening at his home while his
parents were away. I was fortunate enough to be on the invite
list. There were the usual: the boobs, the moans, the flirty talk,
the jizz, but I felt no joy. I felt wearing dresses was superior. I
felt content with dresses when all my classmates were chasing girls. But around the boys, I felt abnormal. This feeling
lingered.

In the blink of an eye, I turned eighteen, I had become
an adult male, I got a new ID card, and on it, in a prominent
location, the letter M. I had reached a milestone, and a lot of
classmates had reached a milestone too: losing their virginity.
I grew up in a prestigious boys' school where the mantra was
Best of the best, but I felt weak: I was a teenager with a dick but
zero achievements with it. Classmates made fun of effeminate
boys and virgins.

I had also heard about trans sex workers in Thailand; I
read a news article about a person who stole his neighbor's
silk stockings and was reported to have an ill mind. Was that
how I would end up? Was I ill too? Maybe I should be a normal adult and save myself from veering too much into sexual

deviance, I thought, so I threw away my dresses and asked my mom to sign me up for extracurricular activities. I wanted to get to know girls outside school and lose my virginity.

I came very close two times. First was Joy; we thought on the same wavelength, we lived in our own world of cinemas and art galleries. We saw each other often. One day I walked up to her and asked her to be my girlfriend. Boom. I was rejected immediately as it was so blunt and out of the blue. I was angry and disappointed because friends are supposed to help each other. Why couldn't Joy see the fact that I was trying to get laid just to get rid of my "illness"? Soon after, I met Carrie through a mutual love of theater. Outside theater, we would go on three-hour walks and talk about an infinite number of topics, and it felt genuine and sincere, and our bond felt strong. But my testosterone started doing the thinking again, and I thought the time was ripe to get rid of cross-dressing. I assumed Carrie loved me and that she was dying to sleep with me. Afraid of being rejected again, I decided to let Carrie take the initiative. But after weeks of waiting and nothing, I confessed to Carrie my addiction to masturbating in dresses, hoping to earn some compassion and speed things up. Boom. She still didn't take the initiative and suggest any plans for intimacy. I felt angry and disappointed, again.

I never met them again, and years later I learned that Joy was mugged and killed at gunpoint while traveling, and Carrie was hospitalized for months due to a brain disease; I don't know if she is around now. I had treated them like passersby in my life, but they could have been lifelong soul mates. Soul mates are only assigned to someone by fate, treasures that I disposed of without thought, as if performing an effortless "swipe to delete" action on my phone's contact list.

I entered year two of university, still a confused self-hating virgin, but with my first girlfriend. Thinking back... did I really love her? No. I was a cruel, manipulative asshole who dated her because she showed a strong interest in me and she was a possible stepping-stone for me to lose my virginity and maybe stop thinking about dresses. After a lot of persuasion, we rented a motel room, and I found myself entering an endurance race. Where most guys are sprinters, I was a marathon runner. Two-plus hours to run a marathon, two-plus hours to finish losing my virginity. Well, sort of. When I left the starting line I felt fine, I quickly had the right shape and size, and I put on the safety costume. There was some in-and-out action and pleasurable moaning. But putting "it" inside someone's cavity felt so foreign, the whole experience was like exploring a new planet; there were so many unknowns, and as time passed I got nervous and then I looked at the clock and I was shocked: forty minutes had gone by and I was nowhere near climaxing. I looked at my girlfriend's expression and body language to find any indications that I had done something wrong. But I could not find any clues. While I was searching my tiny brain for answers, I got distracted and went soft. There was a sigh from my girlfriend. Not good. I might have just traumatized her. Sixty minutes had gone by and I had failed to perform. There was an unbearable silence between us. I thought taking a nap would help calm my nerves and then I would wake up and become the sex machine that I was supposed to be. I started breathing exercises to prepare for the nap and closed my eyes, and then my girlfriend spoke: "First-time nervousness?"

"Sorry."

"It's okay." She kissed me and hugged me… and we tried again.

Twenty minutes later, I still felt I was on an unknown planet. Thirty minutes later, I still hadn't returned to Earth. My girlfriend's moans turned from pleasurable to mechanical to bored to silence. I suggested that I finish myself since we needed to check out of the motel room soon. She nodded. I thought about the pretty dresses I once owned and I came. It was a sign that I had trotted down the wrong path, but I was too dumb to notice it.

In the last year of university, a classmate decided to shoot a comedy video for her graduation project, and in it was a role where an ugly guy becomes a cross-dressing model to make ends meet. She was hoping I could act in the role, and I could tell she was worried that I would say no. It took me only a split second to say YES, and my classmate was like, *What? Are you sure? You have to wear makeup, dresses, a bra, and oranges* (inside the bra, obviously), *and it would be shown in front of the whole class!* Well, in my mind I was like, *What? I have a blank acting portfolio and you sensed that I would take this pervy role. The stars must have aligned!* I almost wanted to confess my true desires, but I was afraid I would make things weird and she would alienate me, so I just shut up and went to the shoot. Sadly there were some script changes, so I only got to wear the dresses and oranges and bra for a few hours, but it was the best few hours in my life up to that point. The idea of appearing as a woman in daily life became implanted in my head, but the idea was quickly locked away in the deepest dungeons of my mind, and I spent more golden years of my youth chasing after the illusion that being a gender-conforming man was what would keep me sane.

My mid-twenties went by in a haze. I had a job I'd never liked, I spent my weekends binge-drinking, I shopped for a lot of dresses online, and built up a lot of debt. I dated girls, but I never felt comfortable and I emotionally abused them when I felt stressed out by the burden of playing a straight guy. I slowly found myself in a Jekyll-and-Hyde situation, and both sides were losing. Around twenty-seven, after completely wrecking a girlfriend's heart and almost causing her to lose her job, I moved into a micro flat to be by myself and have more clarity and space to think deeply about my own struggles, and more importantly, to have the freedom to express myself however I wanted. I wanted to share my struggles with my friends, but I didn't know how; there was nothing in the media about trans issues, aside from farcical roles in soap operas, and even I myself had no idea what I was going through.

The chance for me to be my true self in front of people I love came when a friend decided to have a slumber party. Yes! I brought a blond wig and a silky pink slip to the party, went into the toilet, and changed. I opened the toilet door, walked out like the next supermodel, and posed in front of imaginary spotlights.

There was absolute silence. *Where's the applause and praise?* I had no makeup on. I didn't comb my wig, so it looked like spaghetti. I didn't bother to shave my legs and armpits; the slip was semi-transparent and so small that it could barely cover my ass, and I could feel the pubic hair sticking out of my undies and scratching my thighs.

I totally killed the party mood, my look was raping everyone's eyes, no one spoke to me, but I enjoyed myself. I was being me.

I eagerly waited for the next costume party, and a few months later when the announcement was finally made on Friendster (those were the days), there was this remark in BOLD: ***Beavis*** (my pre-transition name)***, do not wear a dress to a party again!***

I was so pissed because friends were supposed to support me no matter what, so we had a pissing contest on Friendster, I dropped an F-bomb, and my friends fired back: *It's our job to protect our friends and not let them indulge in deviant fantasies!* I denounced them because I needed friends, not discipline masters, and unfriended them all; there was no point hanging around people who had no desire to understand me.

In hindsight, coming out in a trashy semi-nude look didn't help at all. This setback didn't deter me, though, and a few months later there was Halloween. I went out with a new group of friends, wearing a red evening gown, full-on makeup, and a tidy flowing wig. I had shaved everything I could see, so my legs and armpits were smooth as silk. My mates were impressed and they liked me and I had never felt prettier. We went to a club and danced, and suddenly this lonely guy approached me in the darkness and started to initiate some contact with my hips. I was really flattered, and with the booming music and disco lights flashing, it really felt like heaven.

While I was wondering how to treasure this special moment, the alcohol in me guided me toward. I leaned in close to his ear and said, with a voice as deep as the bass coming out of the subwoofers, "Happy Halloween!" He gave me a WTF look and stumbled away.

It was a good night, but I didn't want to share this good night with a drunk guy who probably didn't know what was really going on. All this gave me a great deal of confidence, and I couldn't wait for another chance to be me. I searched online for a cross-dressing group and went to their gathering. I brought the same getup I had for Halloween, thinking if I could seduce a man, it would mean I was pretty up-to-standard. I arrived and walked out like a supermodel—absolute silence. Again! No praise!

Then I heard a bitchy voice behind me: "What's up with your makeup, are you in a Chinese opera?"

I realized my makeup was too white and too red for everyday activities, and this was not Halloween.

"Why are your legs so far apart when you walk? You trying to be gangster or something?"

"You really have to work on contouring, girl, your cheekbones are really masculine!"

I looked around; I paled in comparison to the dozens of perfect princesses around me, and it was obvious I had failed the litmus test, and I wouldn't be passable as a woman, and I had lost the eligibility to wear a dress out in public. It was a truly depressing revelation. I ditched all my women's gear. I went back to staring at the floor, hating how I looked.

I kept going to LGBT gatherings, but I lacked the courage to dress up, thinking I would be judged the same way. One time I met a transwoman, Joanne, and she asked me why I was there. I told her my story and showed her some of my past photos, and she asked me why I didn't dress up even though I was in a safe, supportive environment.

"Because I don't think I am passable."

"Does every woman in the street wear heavy makeup; have long, curly, sexy blonde hair; walk like a model; and look like a princess all the time?" she asked.

I looked at her and realized she wasn't wearing makeup or a silky, lacy dress and high heels.

"Beavis, there is no point in being more feminine than a woman. Just be natural and be what you want to be."

I didn't have to wait for chances or care about eligibility, because I didn't have to be a guy even though I was trained to believe I was one. Like the great Nike mantra, *Just do it!* So I grew my hair longer, bought cosmetics that matched my skin tone, stopped looking for evening gowns, and instead bought dresses that had character and looked cool. I asked for feedback at gatherings, and I listened. Armed with a much improved new look, I had less fear of being rejected, and I stopped believing I wasn't passable. I could celebrate; after being stuck in a cage for three decades, I was liberated. I had been fantasizing I was a man, and I had tried and failed trying to realize this fantasy. All along I had thought I was a failure as a man: splitting up with wonderful women, making dead-end career choices… but in hindsight, these actions gave me the flexibility to prepare myself to become a woman. Instead of a failure, I felt like I was a genius.

I began to dress as a woman full time after I turned thirty-one. It was 2011, menswear no longer emphasized masculinity and trans issues had gone mainstream; it was a good time to come out. I shared my journey at storytelling performances and I was applauded. I felt like a tiny star. People were always saying to me, "I like you, you are so brave, you are great!" I thought I would be equally popular everywhere, so I went to social mixers and tried to make new friends. We'd gather in a circle and make self-introductions; when my turn came, I was so excited as a lot of guys laid their eyes on me. I spoke… and dead air. People got drinks and started to chit-chat. I spoke… and dead air again. The event came to a close; I said goodbye… and there were eager goodbyes! WTF? Was it because I was a girl who knew tech? If my words were so boring, then why the hell were people clapping at the end of my stories? I knew I didn't have the sweetest voice, but did I really need to sound like Betty Boop to be accepted? The answer is, for Hong Kong people, a social mixer is supposed to be a fishing pond for erect fishing rods. So for horny desperate guys who had checked me out in a little black dress, the meaning of the song "I'll Never Fall in Love Again" had changed forever:

What do you get when you kiss a girl?
A pretty girl—with a penis
You'll never fall in love again

A few social mixers later, I started seeing Facebook posts about friends having happy dinners or fun events that I was never invited to: I was blatantly excluded; I had become a freak; I was no longer the tiny bright star on the stage. I got depressed and paranoid; maybe those compliments I got were never real—when they said they liked me, it was only as re-flexive as clicking "Like" on Facebook. Being brave was never an asset. I hid myself, connected to society only through the Internet, and stumbled across the local BDSM scene. The people there truly understood what it felt like to be marginalized, and they became my most ardent supporters; they cheered me on, and I got my groove back.

Time flies. I started psychiatric evaluation (yes, gender dysphoria is part of the healthcare ecosystem) so I could get a referral for sexual reassignment surgery. I took hormones, I felt great, and I even began using the ladies' room in preparation for the evaluation. But then, there was a significant hurdle: the psychiatrist invited my mom to a future appointment.

I rarely saw my mom since I had started living on my own. How was I going to set up this big reveal?

Perhaps fate stepped in. I started to have rectal bleeding, and my doctor told me I had a fistula (something more gory than a hemorrhoid) that required a quick surgery to fix. No problem, in-and-out after one night. However, the doctor neglected to tell me one important piece of information—I could not be discharged on my own. So, the morning after surgery, still groggy from the anesthesia, I was stuck in the hospital room because I hadn't arranged for anyone to come pick me up. Who could come with ZERO notice? Mom. We got in a taxi and she opened the door of my home. Dresses piled up in plain sight. But neither of us said a word. I collapsed on the bed. As she was leaving, my mom asked, with a smile, "Are those dresses yours?"

I could pretend I had a girlfriend and use that as a shield

or I could just be honest, but my brain was too tired to think so I chose the latter. I explained the whole process, and I was expecting her to shut the door and to never see each other again.

"Since I caught you wearing my dress twenty years ago, I had a big question mark in my heart, and I'm glad that I can erase it after all this time. I'll be by your side the rest of the way. You're old enough to make your own decisions and there's no point for me to resist my children's wishes now. Rest up, and tell me the date of the appointment when you are feeling better," my mom said, smiling.

Wow. Not what I expected at all. So I marched on with one more ally. The surgery was scheduled for 10 August 2015, but I needed to check in on the ninth. *What is the extra day for?* I asked myself, but I neglected to ask my sisters who had gone through SRS. So I arrived at the hospital under a cloud, changed into the gown, and was promptly given two two-liter bottles of transparent liquid.

"This is a laxative to clear your bowels. Drink it all within two hours and I need to check that your output is clear like water before I can let you into the operating theater," the nurse said.

Four liters of laxatives? Wasn't that overkill? I started my first cup. *Eeewwwww!* Six hours and ten trips to the toilet later, it was still brown. Two more liters were given to me. Time was running out because I was just twelve hours away from surgery; I huffed and puffed for a few more hours until all the color was gone. It was a close call because they only give out SRS appointments once a month, and if I was forced to miss it because of my poop, I would probably have to wait another year or more. When I was pushed into the operating theater and lifted onto the table, arms and legs spread wide, I was like, "Yeah, give it to me!" and then I was given a gas mask and soon I was asleep.

I woke up some time later facing a bowl of congee and some medical equipment, and nurses were barking important information but I couldn't hear them because I was too focused on feeling down there to see if my penis was still in place. There was something long and hard… what? And then I reached under my gown. Phew, it's just bandages.

The first week I had to be confined to bed, and afterward the bandages would be removed. In pain yet bored to death, I needed something to distract myself, so I turned to Facebook, I took selfies and posted status updates. There were a lot of congrats and comforting words, but one comment haunted me: *Is it elective surgery?*

Elective surgery, like I had asked for it; the whole ordeal, I had just asked for it. It was like a comment to tell me to shut the hell up. *Yeah, it's just elective surgery, it's not life-or-death surgery.* Were people thinking that I was wasting vital resources—would the bags of blood used on me have been better off on a real patient, or was *I* a real patient?

Day seven came, the day of the ribbon-cutting ceremony. I was supposed to rejoice and there would be fireworks, but I was still thinking of the A-hole who said *elective surgery.* The surgeon took off the bandages, and I was introduced to my brand-new vagina. He gave me instructions to care for it using a dilator. I added lube and slowly twisted and thrust it in and it was NOT like a scene in a (mainstream) porno: there was no pleasure and moaning, it was just scary because I didn't know if the sutures would fail and the wound would go BOOM. When I reached the limit, I was very disappointed my dilator didn't go all the way in. I used to have a five-inch Asian penis, which I guess made me average-sized. But now my woohoo was only three inches deep. If a parallel universe version of me tried to have sex with me, it could not accommodate my junk. Shit, it's totally undersized if I want to go international. I have a LOT of unfulfilled dreams, and pimping myself is the ultimate shortcut to these dreams. Having a petite fanny isn't very helpful.

I also had to learn how to pee. The first time I just sat and relaxed and I sprayed all over the floor like a fountain. I knew I had to change my posture and angle to focus the spraying. I sometimes still feel like I have a penis because honestly, the plumbing down there is unchanged.

I was discharged on the tenth day, and my mom came to accompany me home. I was so ready to walk out the exit and into my new life… ouch… ouch… my mom, helpful as ever, noticed and asked with a smile: "Hey, are you ready to be a lady yet? Why are you walking like that?"

"Mom, you know I have a wound the size of your face right? So cut me some slack."

The following weeks recovering at home were another highlight; I was hoping the wound would heal ASAP, but the swelling retreated like one millimeter every week, and then the swelling on the right side decided to retreat faster than the left so I had a weird asymmetrical pussy. There was a lot of yellow gooey stuff flowing around, and it seemed that I had gone through all the trouble just to have a runny lady part with a foul smell. Whenever I stood or walked or sat up, blood would go rushing toward my wound, punching my foot-long sutures like a boxing champion, and I would have to lie down to make the pain stop. One week passed, three weeks passed, five weeks passed, but nothing improved. I thought I had trained up a high level of pain tolerance because I was a little into SM, but an occasional five minutes of being whipped didn't prepare me to face six weeks of constant pain. On top of the pain, when I put a mirror down there, it looked nothing like the many pretty vajayjays I had licked and kissed before; there were just random lumps of raw flesh and pale patches of raw skin. All this time I waited, but my happy place was still a sad place.

Deciding to find something to do to distract myself, I went to a voice-training workshop to sound more feminine. After the first lesson I went home to practice raising my pitch: "Wo... o... wo... o... AHHHHA... Fuck!" I just couldn't do it. If someone cannot sing, they cannot sing. And even if I succeeded with short phrases, how could I maintain the same intensity every waking second for the rest of my life? So was I going to waste all my brainpower just to speak like a woman and do nothing else? What would happen if I had a few rounds of drinks and got too relaxed?

A lot of friends left messages on Facebook offering blessings for my new life, like everything would magically change for the better. Really? Female friends still don't like hanging out with me because I am misleading—misleading guys into thinking that my friends are also transgender. Women won't see me as an equal because I don't have to suffer from periods. Sex from this point forward will probably be BYOT—bring your own toy. I still sweat the same and stink the same, like a guy. I will still be a *persona non grata* at many events... I will be taking synthetic hormones for the rest of my life, and when an integral organic element of my body is replaced by chemicals, who knows how long my liver and body can last? My life probably will suck the rest of the way, but would it be any different than if I had not had the surgery? Would it suck less if the name on my ID card were still Beavis and people continued making butthead jokes? Would life be more wonderful if people only loved me as a guy? Nah. Either way I would have to deal with what other people think. If life has to suck, it sucks in a better way now that I am a woman. So paraphrasing Jay-Z, I have a *Public Service Announcement*:

Allow me to re-introduce myself
My name is Beatrice
And I am the CEO of my L-I-F-E, life
Love me or leave me alone

After I felt well enough to be out and about, the most sensible thing to do would be to insert myself into a Prince Charming romantic fantasy, where a handsome French guy would hits on me with a sexy accent in a classy bar. I would say, "Your place or mine?" and then something censored would happen. Now that I had a girl's body, re-entering nightlife was like discovering a diamond ring in a trash can. Yes, drunk guys rubbed their sweaty bodies against mine, but I was perfectly accustomed to that. I used to play soccer. When I told my friends about such encounters, they got concerned and warned me about protecting my body. But I am proud of my new body. It's a miracle and I want to share it with the world! Nightlife is hard to navigate, especially when it's full of predators, but sometimes I am glad that they put their hands on me instead of some innocent girl who isn't prepared for such sexual harassment, and when I take one for the team, I feel like a hero.

After months of nighttime adventures, at the end of 2015 I went to a friend's fancy dress party, and for the whole night this girl, Kimmy, couldn't take her eyes off me. Her eyes were all lit up. She was totally mesmerized. I tried to avoid her but it was hard because she was a bit... B-I-G. She made her way toward me and started chanting, "You are so pretty." And I was like, *You talking to me?* I wasn't having any fantasies because I felt like she was just into my appearance. She was twenty-one, and I was thirty-five, so we were probably three generation gaps apart.

One day after work I was bored so I went to join my friends for drinks, the same friends who hosted the party where I met Kimmy. And when I showed up after work, it meant I'd be showing you the ugliest side of me—I worked in an IT department at the time, where dressing up and looking good was a sin. At the bar there she was, Kimmy again, eyeing me, and I was thinking yeah, I am going to take this opportunity to knock some sense into her. I took her hand and dragged her to the brightest corner in the bar and chatted in my most relaxed non-gender conforming voice.

"Hey, wassup, welcome to my chemical-free face."

She got very shy and blushed because I touched her hand and she still thought I was the prettiest girl in the room. She was so cute, and I have always had a soft spot for shy people. We chatted, and I was slowly becoming attracted to her, and why not, I used to date girls before. She was so considerate, pure, simple and direct and loving and caring and brave and I can go on forever. When I had to leave early, she gave me a bear hug, and I just felt like a baby bear in her arms. I realized Prince Charming was not who I was longing for: mother bear was. That was the sweetest Wednesday ever.

Thursday, we went on a date, and I learned she taught music—CAREER, tick. Friday we went out clubbing, I learned that she knew Thai boxing and could muscle away drunks who wanted a piece of my ass. I felt so protected—SECURITY, tick. Saturday, I was in love and we were holding hands and kissing and tongue-fucking and it felt like a fairy tale. Sunday, I woke up hoping to spend the best Sunday in my life ever with my first true love, but I got some bad news: her family is Christian, and she has to go to church with her family every Sunday, so every week I spent six wondrous days and end the week on a very depressing note. Over many lonely Sundays, I spent the days weighing the pros and cons of dating Kimmy.

PRO: She is full of love when we are dating.

CON: Her parents will give us shit if they know we are dating.

PRO: She has a good heart and is close and honest with her parents, so she tells them she is dating.

CON: She tells them she is dating Jason.

OMFG.

So we had to think about how to build a cover for Jason. Okay, I have the voice of a Jason. What if her parents bumped into us on the street? Okay, *Hi, parents, I have a cross-dressing problem, and my job is...* Hey! Why the fuck did I have to go back to pretending to be a guy? Hadn't I wasted enough years doing this already?

And I got more bad news: I would have to spend Christmas and New Year alone because her parents were taking her on a trip to Australia. Their annual tradition. But it was okay, we could Skype—but only for five minutes each day when Kimmy was hiding in the toilet. And I'd just spend the rest of the holidays on the street walking amongst sweet and loving couples. Kimmy would send me a text every day reminding me it's only ten days, but it's not okay when it's THOSE ten days EVERY year. And even if she were in Hong Kong, our time together would be spent looking over our shoulders, or with Kimmy worrying that she would miss messages or calls from her parents. I don't know what crime I committed; I only wanted to be cared for and loved like a normal person, but I ended up living like a fugitive. If only her parents could judge us with blindfolds on like JUSTICE, then we would be safe because I could still sound like a guy—but no, not happening. The math just didn't add up: a transgender plus a non-Christian, plus two lesbians, plus a Christian home is an unsolvable equation. No matter what I did, the result would be the same:

Religion: one

Our homosexual love: nil

And then after Boxing Day, on a blue Monday, I did it: I dumped Kimmy via a two-thousand-word text message because it was the right thing to do. Kimmy did not reply; there were just blue ticks letting me know she had read it. I proceeded to wish her luck in her future relationships, I told her to be careful when hooking up with strangers, and as I kept typing this advice, I felt that I really loved her. Just hours after I texted *I am dumping you*, I texted *I really love you.*

Kimmy finally texted back: *WTF? R u fucking playing me?*

And... I... I said it's a mistake... It's the hormones messing with my mind.

We sort of reconciled, and we both thought we should have a face-to-face to sort things out right after she landed in Hong Kong. On 2 January, we met up; I put on my sweetest smile and held her hands tight, thinking that that message was history. Then I looked at her, her blank face, her cold lifeless hands just hanging there, and I realized, to her, it was not just a text message, it was a scar. A scar I caused because I was trapped in meaningless assumptions.

"What are we now?" she asked me. "Anything BUT girlfriends?"

There was silence. Dumping someone is not something you can undo. I knew that no literary genius could salvage this moment, so I closed my eyes and threw a Hail Mary:

"We are lovers now. I am sorry about Australia. But I know I really love you and want you. Will you forgive me?"

She replied with a death stare, and then threw me a curveball: "If we are lovers, why haven't you kissed me?"

I kissed her passionately, and she responded by taking out her phone and forcing me to explain my stupid two-thousand-word breakup text line by line, but hand in hand. OMG, that was the sweetest embarrassing thing ever, and I just knew she was the one, even though there would be many more lonely Sundays to come, even though her parents would always be a threat. I was in love and I didn't care. Love is just a bunch of strong sensations, and sensations never make any sense.

However, old habits die hard. On the surface, I had a good run, a successful surgery, a white-collar job, a loving partner, a small but cozy home. Well… I was the only girl and one of the younger ones in the whole aging IT department. I didn't mesh well with the old guard, and I was isolated and disregarded at work. The ever-changing nature of the IT world made me anxious every day, and I began to have insomnia. Kimmy tried her best to make me feel better at work. She joined me for lunches; she picked me up after work; she cheered me up on weekends.

Once her family began tightening their grip, as they thought she was spending too much time dating, the relationship became a ticking time bomb, and I began to emotionally abuse her. I kept calling her my lovely fat penguin when we hugged, and I liked to play with her big tummy. I never perceived it as fat-shaming but to her it was. I would have a meltdown when I prepped for her birthday. I kept sending her two-thousand-word breakup and not-breaking-up text message threads whenever I felt lonely on weekends.

I forced her to make an incoherent short film with me because I had a premonition that I could be a successful filmmaker and I would win awards with it. The process was brutal. I had no idea what I was doing and I kept losing my temper when things went wrong, and it happened every minute throughout the production because I never had the training or skill set to be a filmmaker; I was just fuelled by a delusion. Awards never came of course, and I checked out from reality. I drank more, I started smoking, I took recreational drugs, I went clubbing alone weekly against Kimmy's wishes. Our rift grew wider and even though she gave me a lot of signs, I still felt blindsided when she broke up with me at the end of 2017.

I cracked, I quit my job, I stayed at home for months, I cut off contact with friends and family. And then I talked to my psychiatrist about the whole saga. What I thought was a dent in my psyche as a result of the breakup was just a small fleck in the whole dark picture. In the past, I was able to mask my signs of depression and anxiety because I was singularly focused on my transition; no one noticed anything wrong because I still had a good sense of humor when I faced rejections and failures, and girlfriends thought my psychotic breaks were just lovers' quarrels.

There were times when I could have taken the easy way out, but fate had other plans: I continually found new friends and opportunities that kept me going. I guess that is what happens when you live in a crowded city like Hong Kong; it's so dense that it's hard to not bump into hope.

Dedicated to David Young (RIP) and Hong Kong Stories.

"ARE YOU MARRIED?" IS NOT A YES OR NO QUESTION

By Nancy L. Conyers

W HEN my spouse, Libby, was offered a new position last year based in Singapore, we were thrilled. We had previously lived in Shanghai, Hong Kong, Italy, and Sweden, and after five years in Europe we were more than happy to be going back to Asia, to a country where we could brush up on our rusting Mandarin and eat great Chinese and Indian food. We weren't happy, though, about moving to a city-state where our marriage wasn't recognized, where Section 377A of the penal code criminalizes sex between mutually consenting adult men but says nothing about women. And, most importantly, to my thinking, says nothing at all about love, suggesting that same-sex relationships are only about sex. Once again, our relationship, our marriage, and our love were going to be invisible.

*

The move to Sweden was the first time in almost eleven years of living abroad that we moved to a country officially as a married couple. On the resident-visa application form where it asked, *What are the circumstances of your move to Sweden?* I don't have words to describe the utter joy I felt ticking the married box and writing, *I am a trailing spouse.* I was an official trailing spouse and there was none of the anxiety or deliberation about what we should say about our relationship and marital status that we'd experienced in every other location. When the caseworker read our applications, she asked to see our marriage license, made a copy of it, and said, "Welcome to Sweden." Simple as that. My eyes welled up and I wasn't even able to choke out a thank-you. That moment was so huge for me, and for Libby and me, but it was just another moment in a typical day for that Swedish caseworker.

The feeling of freedom we had in Sweden—the freedom to just say yes when someone asked if we were married, the freedom of no automatic assumption that being married meant being married to a man, the freedom of openly walking down the street and holding hands—warmed up those long and dark Swedish winters considerably.

*

Even though we are married, every time Libby and I move internationally and fill out our paperwork for our visas, we have to stop, think, and decide which box we should tick when it comes to the question of *Are you married, single, divorced, or widowed?* The question, *Are you married?* is not a yes or no question for us. It depends on which country we're moving to and living in, what the laws or cultural norms are in that country, and how our answers will affect Libby's ability to do her job, my ability to come and go as I please and not be turned away at the border or interrogated about my comings and goings, and our ability to live our long-term married life together.

*

When Libby and I made our commitment to each other in 1988, there were no protections for gay people in the United States, either individually or as a couple. We weren't able to legally marry, so we moved in together and privately vowed to be there for each other for better or for worse. While we were happy, we also felt diminished. Sitting on the floor eating pizza, clinking our slices together and saying, "We did it," wasn't the wedding or reception either of us had imagined for ourselves. We felt married even though we legally weren't.

In August of 2013, for our twenty-fifth anniversary, Libby and I were finally able to have the wedding of our dreams. I'd been planning this wedding down to every last detail in my head the whole time we'd been together, but what I hadn't planned on, what we hadn't known, was the surge of feelings and emotions and love that would envelop us as we began walking down the aisle together. It was overwhelming and made up for having to wait twenty-five years for that moment. The night was truly magical, one where we felt like we were floating inside the dream we had long ago conceded would never, ever happen. Yet, there we were, declaring our love for each other openly, legally, clinking champagne glasses in front of the people we loved most in the world instead of clinking slices of pizza by ourselves.

*

The year 2004 was a watershed year for us because we moved to Shanghai, our first international assignment after moving domestically to different locales. We were now officially called expatriates. This was the first move we'd made where I was also officially a domestic partner, allowed on the company health insurance plan, and fully included in all the move preparations. Everyone in human resources and upper management at Libby's company knew about me, which was a wonderful feeling, but the irony was that we were explicitly told not to say anything to anyone about our relationship. China had no laws against gay people, but there were no laws protecting us either. Since the company was jiggering around with my visas because we couldn't move on a family visa like the other expats, they felt it was important to keep quiet about our relationship. Looking back on that now, it seems crazy that we agreed to those conditions, but at the time we just wanted to move to Shanghai so badly. Libby is half Chinese and had always wanted to explore the Chinese side of herself. We also wanted to see if we could find out what had happened to her Chinese grandfather during the Cultural Revolution, and find the grave of my missionary ancestor who was buried near Ningbo, a city outside of Shanghai.

Even though China was the most fascinating place we've ever lived, and Shanghai is the most incredible city in the world, where my heart will continue to live for the rest of my life, the stress of having to be closeted took its toll. We, of course, didn't keep completely quiet and made decisions about who to tell and who not to tell, but now that we're not there anymore, I realize the day-to-day anxiety I lived with. Every time there was an unexpected knock at the door, I jumped.

After living in Shanghai for four years, my luck ran out. I was hauled into the immigration police and questioned two times, purposely separated from the human resources director of Libby's company who had accompanied me. It wasn't my gayness or our relationship that caused me to be questioned, it was the fact that I'd had thirteen F visas over that four-year period. F visas were short-term visas lasting anywhere from thirty days to six months that Libby's company had sponsored for me. Essentially, her company was inviting me to do business with them and providing me with a visa to do so, even though I never provided her company with any business services. As China began preparing for the 2008 Summer Olympics in Beijing, the Chinese government decided that foreigners would cause trouble and would protest human rights violations that would garner international coverage. Any foreigner who'd had numerous F visas like I'd had was suspect.

Thankfully, the human resources director of Libby's company, who'd been sent to the countryside to work on a pig farm during the Cultural Revolution and who was skilled at being interrogated, was able to smooth things over with my questioner. The interrogator had a file almost six inches thick on me, and he was convinced that I was either a tax evader or an American spy because there was no logical explanation for why I'd spent so much time in China since we were forbidden from saying anything about our relationship. I was told to leave China, and I'm guessing that this was so my interrogator could save face with his superiors and report that one more "bad" foreigner was made to leave China before the Olympics began.

The human resources director of Libby's company knew exactly how to handle my interrogator and was able to get him to tell her how I could return. As we were leaving, my final interrogation my questioner pulled the human resources director aside and told her to tell me to get a new passport with a new number in my home country after the Olympics ended and apply for a tourist visa to return, which I did. I eventually got back into China, but it was never the same. I felt as if I was living on borrowed time. Shortly after I returned to China, another company recruited Libby for a job that was based in Hong Kong. We jumped at the chance to move to the city that, while part of China, was easier to navigate visa-wise for me and was the city where Libby grew up.

*

In the Asian countries and city-states we've lived in, I find it infuriating to not have my marriage recognized. It's infuriating to watch straight expat men lose their boundaries, behave badly, cheat on their wives, and reinforce the stereotype of the "sexpat" while I have to remain silent, and our stable, loving, long-term marriage remains invisible and even looked down upon.

*

Being back in Asia, in Singapore, means I'm back to being an unofficial and invisible trailing spouse. I'm coming in and out of Singapore on a Social Visit Pass, which allows me, as an American, to stay in Singapore for eighty-nine days without a visa, then I need to leave for five days. I'm mindful every time I leave and come back that I could be denied entry. I'm mindful not to stay longer than sixty days and to stay out for longer than five days so I don't arouse interest in my movements. I'm mindful that same-sex relationships are not recognized under the law in Singapore and that no anti-discrimination protections exist for LGBT people here.

It only took a year for my luck to run out in Singapore, though. As I was leaving last month to come back to the U.S. for a few weeks, I was pulled aside by an immigration official who took me to be questioned by his supervisor.

"What is the nature of your visits to Singapore?" the supervisor asked me.

"I'm not sure I understand what you mean," I responded. After the interrogations in Shanghai, I've learned to hold my ground and give nothing away.

She proceeded to tell me, "We notice you come quite frequently to Singapore. Why is that?" I very sunnily explained to her that since I'm retired, I've been traveling in Southeast Asia. I said that if she'd seen I was coming frequently to Singapore, she could probably also see that I travel to other places as well.

"Have I overstayed my visit?" I asked her, knowing full

well I hadn't.

"You always stay at the same place," she responded, "Who are you staying with?"

"A friend," I replied. Underneath I was simmering having to call Libby "a friend."

The supervisor told me that my visits were quite unusual, that most Americans only stay up to forty-five days, stamped my passport, then sent me on my way.

While nothing like the interrogations in China, this exchange was unnerving. The immigration supervisor unknowingly indicated to me what I needed to do in the future—not stay more than forty-five days. She also made me realize that I can't keep relying on the Social Visit Pass to enter and exit Singapore, so right now I'm staying in the U.S. for six to eight months, away from the prying eyes of Singapore and away from my spouse. Along with Libby's company, we are coming up with contingency plans for how we go forward. There are options we are exploring and hopefully one of them will work out so that we can have our life back together in Singapore.

*

Libby and I celebrated our thirtieth anniversary in August. I said in my wedding vows that I'm not only proud that we've stayed together but I'm proud of *how* we've stayed together. We've supported each other's dreams, given each other the space to grow and change, and have worked side by side building our life together. I come home to a house that is filled with love, respect, and laughter, a home where we talk to each other about what is really going on in our lives and about how we really feel. A home where we listen to each other and honor each other. If that isn't a marriage, I don't know what is.

I'd like to come home to a house in Singapore that I don't have to keep leaving, where I can stay as long as I'd like. Though I may not like it, I've learned to live with what comes with being an unofficial trailing spouse. I have to do what I have to do to keep my family together and I pine for the day anywhere in the world when I am asked if I'm married I can simply say, "Yes."

ALL THE WAYS TO SAY I'M GAY

By Aaron Chan

At seven years old, in the third grade

Like all the other primaries (kindergarteners to third grad-ers), we were sprinting and chasing each other like feral an-imals during recess and lunch. In those days (and probably still today), at my elementary school located in my hometown, Vancouver, British Columbia, Canada, there were always in-sults at any moment, even if we didn't know what they truly meant. Someone mentioned these words, one by one, and like many other taboo grown-up words, we whispered them with cupped hands into beckoning ears, spreading them like germs.

On this particular day, the word was "GAY!"

Everyone was shouting it—and all its variations—at each other like rocks flung from slingshots, hoping to playfully bruise: "You're gay!" "You're gayer!" "You're sooooooo gay, you're the gayest!" Even at seven years old, I knew I liked other boys, but I never knew there existed any sort of word for it. So, when I asked a classmate what this "gay" thing meant, she told me it was when boys like other boys, and girls like other girls. It also meant happy, but that wasn't nearly as fun as the other meaning.

I had finally found the word I could use to describe myself. And it was such a nice word too: It also rhymed with "Yay!" which was quite an enjoyable expression to say.

While the other kids squealed and screamed to whatever game they were playing, I skipped around the woodchip-softened playground on my own, gleefully announcing, "I'm gay! I'm gay!" to no one / everyone / mostly myself. Nobody seemed to care (or hear me); no one laughed or stared or wanted to beat me up.

I was so elated and excited to express this newfound revelation to everyone that when I spied the adult supervisor sitting on one of the pale blue benches, I just had to tell her too. I snuck up behind the woman as quietly as a giddy kid possibly could, then leaned in and said into her ear, "I'm gay"—quite gaily, I might add.

Before she could do anything, I frolicked away, amazed at my own boldness; unfortunately, I heard her calling to me from behind, ordering me to stop and come back. I attempted to avoid confrontation with her by conversing with my friend Jessica, who conveniently happened to be nearby, but the supervisor didn't let up. She approached me, and being the adult-fearing youngster I was, I gave her my attention.

"Where did you hear that word?" she demanded, her face stone serious. "The only meaning for that word is happy. It doesn't mean anything else. Don't you ever think it means anything else. Do you understand?"

As she lectured me, tears escaped from my eyes. By the time she asked that final question, all I could do was manage a slight nod. She dismissed me, and I ran off to the bathroom, a blubbering mess, wondering why and how this strange lady thought she knew me better than I knew myself.

It would be another ten years before I was able to physi-cally say the word again.

*

At fourteen years old, to my diary
The idea terrified me for days.

I didn't want anyone to know, but at the same time, I wanted—no, needed—someone to know. So, after mulling it over, when the slits of light underneath the doors of my mom's and sister's rooms flicked off to darkness, I locked my bedroom door and knelt in front of the big drawer on the left side of my desk. Sticking nearly my entire arm in, I groped around used binders and my clarinet gear before locating the notebook I had stashed months ago.

I opened it to the next blank page and took a seat at the desk. With a black fine-tip pen in hand, I let out a slow, mea-sured sigh as the trembling pen hovered above the page.

Not knowing where to begin, I started with small talk.

Jan. 6, 2003
     Happy New Year! I went snowboarding at Whistler Blackcomb. It was so fun! Jessica got stuck in a ditch and we couldn't find her for about fifteen minutes. To the important news now: The depression is really taking its toll. I'm so close to killing myself.

Okay, enough delay. Get to it. Now. I steadied my hand and gripped the pen harder.

> To add to my misery, my crush on Sean Dwyer has got
> me hallucinating what life would be like if he was my boy-
> friend. I'm so scared to tell anyone I'm

I couldn't write it. *It's just a word, an arrangement of letters,*
I rationalized, but it wasn't enough because they weren't simply letters or strokes of black ink. That three-letter word was
too big, too powerful—I couldn't even say it aloud. Besides
being a confession, it was a bomb, waiting to explode in the
eyes of whoever read this. I glanced at the still-locked door,
then around my room as if my ancestors, in their ancient silk
robes and peasant work clothes were looking over my shoulder, invisible, waiting to see how the sentence would end. This
bedroom could so easily not be my room anymore just by the
act of pressing this quivering pen to the lined paper of this
book.

But for my sanity, I must.

> I'm so scared to tell anyone I'm gay because I keep thinking
> that they won't accept me for the way I am. And now, if by
> some weird reason I ask Sean if he can be my boyfriend, I'm
> so afraid he'll reject me for the way I am. Then, he'll tell every-
> one that I'm gay and then I'll have no friends and everybody
> will think of me differently.

My hand lifted off the page for a second, letting the wild
thought of my mom snooping around my room and stum-

bling upon my notebook interrupt me.

If someone reads this, my life will be ruined.

*

At fourteen years old, to Aunt Wendy[1]
From: Aaron Chan
To: Aunt Wendy
Date: Sept. 6, 2003
Subject: The Secret Confessions of Aaron Chan

Dear Aunt Wendy,

How are you? I am okay, I guess up till today. My mom is forcing me to go to Air Cadets[2] for another year, starting this Monday. This sounds like I'm insane but I really need your help.

Last year, when I was in Cadets, I became very depressed and moody all the time. I tried to tell my mom I had been going through depression but she didn't know what that was.

[1] When I was younger, I thought Aunt Wendy, who lived in Hawaii, was the cool relative in my family. She was the youngest aunt (whereas my mom was the eldest), spoke the best English, and was probably the most liberal/Westernized. I used to call her up and chat with her about school and life because I felt like she understood me miles more than my more conservative parents.

[2] Air Cadets is a program for (mostly unwilling) teenagers that meets weekly. During meetings, we learned and did marching drills, listened to dry lectures delivered by other, higher-ranked cadets (who were also teenagers; one class was all about hygiene and the importance of brushing one's teeth and showering. Yes, seriously), and occasionally travelled out to an airstrip and flew small planes/gliders. Think Boy Scouts but less focused on survival skills and more on aviation. I had no interest in any of these activities, not to mention I felt like sometimes the older kids would abuse their authority. One time, one of them yelled at me for not saluting a group of officers as I walked by, something I didn't know I had to do (plus, the officers were talking amongst themselves and didn't notice me). But this guy scolded me anyway—very condescendingly, I might add. He told me to write a letter to these people apologizing for being disrespectful and to give it to them next week. I never wrote it.

I figured it was useless anyways, since I tried many times before and she still wouldn't change her mind. I started to think about taking my own life. I know this sounds crazy and that it's out of my character, but it is true. I really believed that it was the only way for me to get what I wanted, but of course there was something that stopped me. It wasn't school, grades, siblings, or anything out of the ordinary. I had a crush on someone at my school. For the past year, they were the only thing holding me back from stupid decisions, like suicide. I wondered why I gave into things so easily. If I didn't have a crush, I might not be here today, though I am not quite sure.

When my mom first promised me and Maggie[3] that we'd only spend a year at Cadets, I breathed a sigh of relief. I know she wants me to get a good job in the future, but she just sticks me in a course and expects me to like it. That is really mean.

This is my final plea. I don't know what else to do. I would like you to talk to my mom or something, to try and convince her to let me stop going to that terrible place. If she hears it from you, she may just change her mind. Tell her what I just told you, except for the crush part. I don't want her to know about that just yet. If you are still unconvinced that I am telling the truth, I can't say anything else. If you do not do anything, that's your decision. But you might wake up and find your "favorite" nephew is gone.

Love, Aaron

From: Aunt Wendy

---

[3] My twin sister, older by five minutes.

To: Aaron Chan
Date: Sept. 7, 2003
Subject: Re: The Secret Confessions of Aaron Chan

Dear Aaron, my favorite nephew,

I am very concerned about your well-being and can only imagine the pain you must have suffered in the last few years. As soon as I finished reading your email, I telephoned your mommy and told her about your plea for help, except the crush you had on someone at school. At first she was stubborn, but as I explained to her your depression and thoughts about suicide, she began to listen.

Basically she wants you and Maggie to learn something outside of school. She thinks that you and Maggie have a lot of idle time on hand, and are wasting precious time on the weekend by sleeping in late, etc. Are you willing to go to learn another thing, say, at Chinese school, or swimming, or Boy Scouts, to offset not having to go to Cadets?

As for the person you had a crush on, what happened?

I hope you will stay focused in school but feel free to email me if you need to talk to someone or have any questions about relationships or life. I will try my best to talk to you.

Take care.

Love, Auntie Wendy

From: Aaron Chan
To: Aunt Wendy
Date: Sept. 7, 2003

I'm glad you phoned my mom. She negotiated with me after your phone call and I have to find another course outside of school to replace Cadets, but if I don't, then I must go back there again. Right now, I am so relieved that I get to choose something else. As for my crush, I still like them but I just have one question: How do you know the difference between a crush and when you're in love?

Love, Aaron

From: Aunt Wendy
To: Aaron Chan
Date: Sept. 8, 2003

Dear Aaron,

I am glad your mom listened to your plea. As for the difference between having a crush and falling in love, there is a BIG difference.

Let me use myself as an example. When I was seventeen, I had a crush on my history teacher. I wondered where he lived, if he had a girlfriend, how many siblings he had, what kind of food he liked, etc. You name it, I wondered. I would sit up straight and listen to his teaching every class. When I saw him in the hallway, I would address him and hoped he would remember me. My interest in him was of course not returned and not noticed. In a few months, my interest in him or feelings for him went away, and I even wondered why I was interested in him in the first place. There were no broken hearts, no tears, and no sleepless nights because the feeling was one-sided, silly, yet perfectly normal for a teenager. That is called a crush.

Aaron, it is perfectly normal to have a crush on someone you meet. At first glance, that person may seem so nice and so perfect; however, it is more important to take the initiative to slowly get to know that person, and develop a friendship first. Instead of putting that person on a pedestal, it is very important to get to know her and be her friend first. Most couples become friends first, lovers later.

Not until both parties enjoy each other's company so much that both agree to be exclusive with each other. When that occurs, you are in a relationship and in love. You cannot be in love with someone who is not even aware of your existence or feelings.

Even falling in love has a lot of heartaches, tears, and sleepless nights because a relationship requires a lot of patience, compromise, and sacrifice. More on that later, when you are in love.

Aaron, I know teenage years are very trying and confusing. I am here to do my best to help you through them. I hope I explained myself well.

By the way, why did you use the word "them" when referring to the people you have a crush on? Is there more than one person? Do they know you and have you talked to them?

Talk to you later.

Love, Auntie Wendy

From: Aaron Chan
To: Aunt Wendy
Date: Sept. 8, 2003

Dear Aunt Wendy,

I understood your explanation of a crush and I thought it was good, but it still didn't explain some of the things I felt. There is only one person that I have a crush on, even though I used to like a few people. I used "them" because I think I have a crush on a guy, but I'm not sure.[4] It's really confusing for me right now, with my school life and all, and I might actually be gay. He was in some of my classes last year, and last week, I saw him smoking! And he's only fifteen!!! I have one class with him this year, but we're not really friends and we don't talk to each other. He knows me from last year though, because he was in my French class and he needed help sometimes. I would appreciate it if you wouldn't tell this to my mom because I know she'll flip out and lecture me. My friends say those people like my mom are "traditional" and like everything the old-fashioned way. Anyhoo, I'm really happy about my life, now that I'm rid of all those bad things.

Love, Aaron

From: Aunt Wendy
To: Aaron Chan
Date: Sept. 8, 2003

[4] I was sure. I lied because as liberal as she was, Aunt Wendy was still Chinese and straight, so I believed she wouldn't/couldn't truly understand, that she would tell me it was a phase or that I couldn't know since I was only fourteen.

Dear Aaron,

If the person doesn't even participate in a relationship with you, share the same feelings and emotions as you, it is definitely a crush.

I wonder if you think you are gay because you are curious about what other guys do, compared to you, such as if they play a musical instrument, watch the same movies, like the same subjects, etc., or are you sexually attracted to them, such as, you want to touch and hold them? There is a difference between being curious about other males and being gay. Don't jump to conclusions too soon and label yourself as gay.[5]

If you are not sure whether you are gay at this point, don't think about it. Just concentrate on school, and in a few years, things will look clearer to you.

Also, are you attracted to girls in your school? Not all girls are like Florrie[6], Maggie, and your mom; there are some really decent, sweet, and intelligent girls out there. You will lose out if you don't get to know them. You should hang out with other girls and get to know the opposite sex.

Males and females are good complements of each other as they tend to think and feel differently. Don't close your doors to the opposite sex yet. It is premature to draw that conclusion.

Teenage years are one of the most difficult stages in life because you know a lot more than an adolescent, but yet you don't totally know who you are. In the process of finding who you are, you might become confused about things and peo-

[5] I told you so.

[6] My eldest sister, by nine years.

ple. Don't be afraid. Take your time to grow up and not label yourself so soon.

I am not going to tell your mom about our emails because I want to listen to what you feel and think, then share my personal experiences with you, and hopefully provide some advice to you in the next few years.

Feelfreetoaskmeanyquestions.Iwillbeveryhonestwithyou. Love, Auntie Wendy

From: Aaron Chan
To: Aunt Wendy
Date: Sept. 9, 2003

Dear Aunt Wendy,

I understand about having a crush, but I really can't get him out of my head and when I saw him smoking, I really wanted to go over and yell at him for being so stupid. Every time I see his face, it makes me feel good, which sounds really weird… Also, he never really talked to me before until I helped him a bit in French class last year and then after that he talked to me a bit but this year, I only have one class with him and he has his own friends. I guess you could call him one of the stereotypical Caucasian guys you would find in every high school, who skateboards and stuff like that.[7] I have friends

[7] In addition to the stereotypical North American high school cliques—jocks, nerds, cheerleaders, etc.—skateboarders also had their own group. At my high school, most of them weren't that bright (or maybe they pretended they weren't to fit in with each other), swore often, may or may not have been athletic, and were occasionally boisterous during classes. I don't think Sean was into skateboarding as much as some of the other guys, but he was all the other things I mentioned. And one more thing: When I said he was "stereotypical," I didn't mean it as an insult. It was just a shorthand to efficiently and succinctly describe him to Aunt Wendy, who'd know the type. Besides,

that are girls but I don't really like any girl particularly at my school. I like them as friends but not in a love way. What do you think my mom would say if I told her I liked guys?

Love, Aaron

From: Aunt Wendy
To: Aaron Chan
Date: Sept. 10, 2003

Dear Aaron,

Whatever you decide to do, tell or not tell your mom, DO NOT tell people at school that you might be gay. You might be bullied, verbally abused, or attacked by "traditionists." Be careful because gay people have been attacked and some have even got killed in other cities. It might not be wise to come out of the closet now especially you are still young and confused.

One more thing. The Caucasian you like now. Do you like him for his physical appearance or his athletic skills? Maybe it is admiration instead of attraction. Do you understand the difference between the two? Maybe you wish you had a big brother to protect and care about you, so you prefer being around males.

Anyway, don't jump to conclusions too soon and concentrate your energy on schoolwork.

Love, Auntie Wendy

---

he wasn't a stereotype to me. He was different and handsome and actually intelligent (if only he applied himself!).

*

At fourteen, to my friends Chelsea and Ann

During the summer between the end of Grade 9 and the start of Grade 10, I made plans to hang out with my friends. Although school was out for the season, we decided to meet at our high school because I guess we thought it was cool or something.

This is going to be the day, I thought as I got off the bus and walked across the lush green field to the two figures waiting down the hill for me. I had rehearsed the words in my head for days. Just two words. How hard could it be?

"Where's Lily?" I asked Ann and Chelsea. "And Joanne?"

Ann and Chelsea told me they couldn't make it.

I had hoped to come out to all four of them, but maybe starting with two was a better idea after all.

"I have something to tell you," I told my friends.

"Okay. What?"

As they waited for my revelation, I suddenly became too aware of the situation: I was going to tell them my secret that I vowed I would never disclose to anybody. And what if they told everyone, like it always happens in books? I could get bullied and no one would help me and I could have my face stuffed into a toilet in the boys' washroom and then I'd have to switch schools and oh my god what am I doing?

The words lodged in my throat, and I more or less just stared back, slack-jawed.

"I… can't say it," was all I managed to utter.

"You can't do that!" they exclaimed. "If you don't tell us,

we'll make you tell us!" Then, they proceeded to chase me around the field, but I was a former track-and-field athlete, so their efforts were all in vain. When we were all out of breath, we settled beneath the shade of a great maple tree just beyond the chain-link fence of the school tennis courts.

"So, what the hell is it?" Chelsea began the interrogation again.

Again, I faltered. But an idea came to me. "Guess."

Ann and Chelsea exchanged glances. "Do you like someone?" Of course that was the first thing they asked.

I thought of Sean Dwyer, my biggest crush in the whole world and said yeah.

Now that that bridge had been crossed, I was sure the next part would be easy—but of course I had completely forgotten how heterosexist society is.

"Is it Megan Fu? Oh! Diane? What about Rachelle? Julia Stahl?"

"No, no, ew, and who?"

The more I denied their list of girls in our grade, the less they seemed to catch on. I had to give them a hint. "You're guessing the wrong *type* of people."

"So what? You want us to name ugly people?" Ann retorted.

"No. Just think about it."

At this point, I was so terrified and embarrassed that they would get it that I put my red baseball cap on my face because I didn't want to see their expressions when they guessed right, and I didn't want them to see mine. After some thought, I heard one of them ask quietly, "Do you like men?"

Suddenly, I felt like throwing up. "Yes," I choked. A brief moment of silence followed[8], and I braced myself for their reactions while gulping warm, moist air beneath the cap on my face.

"That's cool. I've always wanted a gay friend," Ann assured me. "We should go shopping!"

"Yeah, it doesn't change anything," Chelsea added. They promised I could trust them with my secret. After a while, when my pulse returned to normal, I almost felt silly for believing my friends might react badly.

"So who do you like?"

"Guess."

Groans followed, then laughter.

"It's a good thing you told us and not Lily or Joanne," they mentioned after, as we walked together to the bus stop. "They're not as liberal as us."

*

At fifteen, to my mom

Four days before my sixteenth birthday, I was sitting on my bed, cradling a guitar on my leg. An instructional book with extra large pink musical notes for beginners was spread on the covers of the bed in front of me.

Knock, knock. Without waiting for an answer, my mom walked in and took a seat on the bed beside me. Wordless entries into my room meant the most serious of talks from my

---

[8] I learned two years later that during this time, Chelsea was apparently stuffing her mouth with bread to keep from laughing—not because the news was hilarious, but because it was so unexpected. Or so she claimed.

mother. I braced myself for whatever was coming.

I couldn't hold her gaze, and had to stare down at the book. Instead of the usual Cantonese she spoke to me with, she said, "I want you to tell me the truth," in measured, calm English, which she only reserved for the gravest discussions. "Are you gay?"

Yesterday, one of my sisters had caught me watching gay porn yet again on the computer. I assumed she told my mom.

I had never thought about how I wanted to come out to my mom, but I didn't imagine it would happen like this. I am a CBC—a Canadian-born-Chinese. Vancouver was the only home I had ever known, the only place I had ever lived. Some labeled me as white-washed. (I didn't.) My parents, on the other hand, were immigrants from Asia (my mom from Hong Kong and my dad from China). My mother's English was rudimentary while she was fluent in Cantonese. She read Chinese newspapers, watched Chinese television shows, prayed at a Buddhist temple. In my eyes, she was still very much culturally Chinese. And though she had never said anything overtly anti-gay, at least to me, I knew that it was a taboo subject and that the Chinese view of homosexuality was unfavourable, to say the least.

Like my coming-out to Chelsea and Ann, saying yes was much easier than saying I'm gay. So I said yes and continued to avert my eyes, now examining the polished wooden surface of the guitar. I could almost hear her mind churning, working up a response.

"You know this is not normal."

Having come across this argument plenty of times in

gay-themed YA novels I had been reading in the past year, I argued, almost like a script, that it was actually normal, that there were animals out there which prove homosexuality was natural. She countered, "Who wants their child to be gay?"

I recalled a quote from Alanis Morisette in an edition of *Xtra West*, the local LGBT newspaper I secretly read. Morissette had mentioned that she'd love to have a child who was gay, because she or he would be that much more special. I didn't think my immigrant Chinese mother would care what Alanis Morissette had said or even knew who she was, so I held back on this. I answered with silence instead.

My mom drove her point further when she pointed out that no one in our entire extended family was gay, so how could I be? I didn't have an answer to that (except that perhaps some of them weren't as straight as they seemed), and when I still didn't respond, she asked, "How come you didn't tell me?"

"You wouldn't be happy if you knew. I know you're homophobic." When I looked over at her, she gave me the stare I had come to recognize means she didn't understand the word or phrase I had said. "I know you don't like it," I simplified.

Her eyes looked sad, as if I disappointed her by not trusting and confiding in her, despite the arguments just now about how being gay wasn't normal.

"Well, why don't you try and change yourself?"

"I can't!"

"How do you know?"

"There's nothing to change!"

"Maybe you should go out with one of Maggie's friends."

My sister's friends were also my friends—Chelsea, Ann, Lily. Obviously, they wouldn't want to go out with their (out) gay friend, not that I would even want to date my friends.

"I don't want to go out with them, or any girl. Could you go out with a woman?"

For a change, I rendered my mother mute. Finally, as if aware of the feebleness of the excuse, she replied, "I don't have time to date."

She shook her head in confusion. "I still don't understand why you are gay. What made you this way?" Her face was full of concern, like I had confessed to having a terminal illness.

"Nothing made me this way," I said with a weary sigh. I was exhausted trying to explain myself when it seemed so clear. But my mom wouldn't let it go.

"Is it because of playing piano? You can stop lessons."

"What? No."

"Is it because of that Wicca thing you're into now?"[9]

"No! Mom, it's none of those things. It's just who I am."

Another pause, longer this time. I thought she finally understood.

Then, "Do you want to go see a doctor?"

In the gay teen stories, both fiction and nonfiction that I devoured voraciously and hid from my family, there were some really unsympathetic, ignorant parents out there: They disowned their kids, verbally and physically abused them, sent them to conversion camp—even kicked them out of their

[9] For about two years, I was interested in Wicca and bought a beginner's Wicca kit. I didn't get that serious about it—mostly just simple incantations to feel good about myself, to have a good day, and to eventually find love. I was open about it with my family, but as hard as I tried to explain it to my mom, she never quite understood what it was or what I was doing.

homes. I knew that were I to come out to my parents, they wouldn't take it well, but at least they would never believe the "gay is a disease that needs treatment" misconception. I mean, my immigrant parents were conservative, but I believed—hoped, really—that having lived in Canada for decades would have influenced them to be more liberal themselves. I was sure they weren't of the idea of ultra-traditional families in China I pictured in my mind, ones who, to my limited knowledge of Chinese life due to never having lived in Asia, forced their queer children to marry someone of the opposite sex to save face or simply rejected or disinherited them entirely. I guessed I was wrong.

"I'm not sick! There's nothing wrong with me." It was only then—when I looked up at my mother's knotted face, eyebrows steeply slanting cliffs, with a mixture of concern and incomprehension—that I realized my mother didn't share this belief. She truly did believe there was something wrong with me. And if she thought I had some sort of disease, what else could she believe in? What else could she do to me?

There was something I had to know. Trying to suppress the accumulating heaving in my abdomen, as if my diaphragm was punching upward at my throat, I managed to choke out between the increasing hiccupping sobs, "Do you still love me?"

She answered without hesitation. "Of course I love you. You are my son."

I had never heard her refer to me as her son. I couldn't hold back anymore and I bawled. Tears fell between the strings of the guitar frets and dampened my shirt. I wrapped my arms around my mother, and felt her squeeze me back. We both cried.

*

At eighteen, to my father

"When are you gonna tell your dad?" Chelsea asked me every now and then. I was sure she was only teasing, but the reminders were enough. I did want to tell him, but I knew he was more traditional than my mom. He was the same man who randomly told me and my sisters in the car once that being gay wasn't natural. It also probably didn't help that my dad and I didn't have a very good relationship—or rather, we simply lacked one—since he hadn't been very present for the majority of his children's lives. On another occasion, he had told me how showing affection for one's kids wasn't how he was raised, and how his father was raised, and so on. It wasn't the Chinese way. And included in the Chinese way was hating on the gays.

After lunch with him one day, my dad parked the car down the street where I lived with my mom and sister. I opened with the classic line: "I have something to tell you," before he waited for me to say it. "I'm gay."

It all happened easier than I thought, the word slipping out with some but relatively much less trouble. I hadn't really considered what he would specifically say or do, but I knew it likely wasn't going to be supportive.

"Do you have a boyfriend?"

It stunned me to hear him say that. I interpreted it as

curiosity, a positive response. I told him I didn't.

"Well, I think you know that I already had a feeling. But you are what you are."

Maybe I was wrong about my parents; maybe my mom was actually the more traditional one. Maybe I had a Chinese dad who was cool with his gay son.

A couple of days later, Dad phoned the house. From my bedroom, I heard my mom speaking with him for a bit, and I continued with my homework before the obnoxious voices from the Chinese soap opera in the living room invaded my space. As I got up to turn down the TV's volume, my mom walked in. She handed me the phone with an expression I couldn't read.

"I have some things to say," Dad declared brusquely.

He started off telling me he had been thinking for the past two days about what I told him. "Being gay isn't right," he stated, and proceeded to list the many reasons why. Most of our conversation wasn't a conversation, but rather my dad going off and me bearing it because I was completely unprepared—that, and I had never argued with my father before.

Line after line, the barrage didn't stop: "If you look at wild animals, it's always male and female. They look after their young. It's human nature.

"No one in the entire generation of Chans has ever been gay. So how can you be?

"When you are gay, you have no desire to have a family, no need to plan for the future, so you go out and party and have sex. Then you get diseases like AIDS. That's why young men die so early."

The one time I countered was when he claimed, "You can't have children. You can't pass down the family name."

"I can adopt," I said.

"Adoption isn't the Chinese way."

I immediately thought of Aunt Wendy and her two recently adopted daughters, but didn't mention it.

"Don't tell anyone else that you are gay. Word goes around and people talk. Everyone knows each other."

After several minutes of one voice on the line, there was a pause. "I am disappointed in your choice," he said, concluding the call.

*

From eighteen-ish to twenty-three-ish, Chelsea introduces me to everyone

It usually went something like this:

A nondescript function of some kind—anything from a birthday party to a fundraiser: Lights are dimmed, music plays. Perhaps there are some decorations and signs on the walls. The crowd is mostly YOUNG MEN and YOUNG WOMEN (twenties), dressed in casual clothing. There's a gentle murmur of voices permeating the air. Some hold alcoholic beverages in their hands as they converse with one another.

CHELSEA, friendly and casual, and AARON, introverted and awkward, enter. AARON scans the crowd and the space as CHELSEA spots FRIEND walking by.

FRIEND: Hey, Chelsea!

CHELSEA: Hey! How are you?

FRIEND: Good, good. You?

AARON subtly gives FRIEND the evil eye at the incorrect usage of grammar, who doesn't notice.

CHELSEA: I'm all right. We just got here.

FRIEND notices AARON standing awkwardly there.

FRIEND: Oh, and this is your—

AARON: No, I'm not—

CHELSEA: He's gay!

AARON glances over at CHELSEA as FRIEND looks slightly amused.

Everyone always thinks we're together, but we're not. And I have a boyfriend. Who isn't here.

AARON: Yeah… (*to FRIEND*) I'm Aaron.

FRIEND: I'm Friend. (*to CHELSEA*) Oh, there's Janet. I haven't seen her in, like, forever! I'm just gonna go say hi. I'll see you in a bit, okay?

CHELSEA: Oh, I have to say hi to her later too. Okay, see you.

FRIEND exits.

(*to AARON*) Sorry I outed you. Again.

AARON: That's okay. You do it better than me anyway.

*

In my twenties, coming out to the world
One of the following:

1.

"What's your memoir about?"

"Oh, about growing up in a conservative Chinese family in Vancouver, juggling those two often-conflicting identities, and… uh, yeah."

There's also a third descriptor in there, but even though my mind tells me to just say the damn word, I can't. I've been out (arguably) since I was seven and here I am, now twenty-five, and I can't tell a curious stranger about the basic premise of my work (I'm pretty sure she would've even found it interesting, given that she seems like a typical, open-minded East Vancouver hippie, dressed in a flowy, earth-toned hemp dress, with long, braided, beaded hair; and that she talks with a slow, soothing drawl). And yet, not a week prior, I had written a book proposal for a creative writing class about my memoir, confidently touting the unabashed gayness of it as a unique perspective and selling point.

"Well, that sounds pretty interesting," hippie chick says.

I smile and nod, believing no doubt that she's unimpressed and only saying that to be polite. I'm left to wonder if I'll be able to properly pitch my memoir when it gets published.

2.

"So, how's your love life?" I'll ask someone once I feel comfortable enough with him or her. It's my go-to, semi-joking phrase. They usually laugh, give a short answer ("Good" or "Non-existent"), and as expected, ask me the same question.

"Oh, my love life is fine. But back to you, how did you two meet?" I'll say. Most of the time, people see through the deflection ruse and only when they press on do I relinquish more details.

"We met online… It's been a couple years now… *He* graduated in kinesiology." Then I brace for their reply, my eyes locked onto their faces for any signs of a negative reaction: a grimace, a tight pursing of the lips, the furrowing of the eyebrows. But there is never any of that. It's always met with neutrality.

"Oh, kinesiology, that's interesting. Did you get to see each other a lot while you were in school?"

I'm left to wonder why I ever built things up in the first place.

3.

"Let's start with Aaron's piece, 'The Birth and Death of You and Me'. What did you enjoy about it?" Andreas Schroeder addresses the class sitting cramped in a circle around wooden tables.

There's a brief moment of silence, which my mind translates as, *Nothing. Everyone hated it and it doesn't even work as a memoir piece. You totally blew someone to get into the program, right? Because there's clearly no other way you should be here.*

Kathleen starts. "As a straight woman, I found it really relatable, even though the piece is about the narrator's awful sexual experience."

I exhale audibly, and some glance my way. My classmates discuss the piece like every other piece in our creative nonfiction workshop class at the University of British Columbia. I figured I had to come out to them at some point if I'm going to be writing about myself, so why not get it over with?

I'm not sure I even came out in person to any of my classmates during my time at university; the overwhelming majority of the material I wrote was so gay—in every genre, not only nonfiction—I simply let it out me by implication. Through this piece right now, I've come out to you.

Now, whenever I write about anything involving gay things (including myself), I feel like I'm channeling that seven-year-old, the one who had the balls to proudly and effortlessly declare his sexuality and shout, "I'm gay! I'm gay!" to the world and not give a shit who cared.

BANYO

By Krista V. Melgarejo

THE *banyo*, or the bathroom in Tagalog, is probably the most intimate room in a person's house. Like the bedroom, the *banyo* holds the most private details of a person's life. Similar to a lover, not only has it witnessed the stripped-down version of a person in the glory of all their natural vulnerability, but it has also memorized the tiniest details of a person's daily routine. The *banyo*'s upkeep and variety, and the number of items you find inside would most likely tell you something about a person's very personal details such as the length of time it takes for them to get ready and how meticulous they are in performing those little tasks before they leave the house.

While I still do believe in how intimately the *banyo* holds one's secrets, I never imagined that there would come a time that I would dread having to enter one—especially ones that are for public use.

I never had a problem with using public restrooms. I had always judged the pleasantness of my experience based on the restroom's upkeep, as I went in and out of the room as I pleased and needed.

That is, up until these past few years.

You see, I'm not exactly what society's stereotypical definition of what a female should look like.

Unlike the majority of biological females, I don't don dresses, skirts, or blouses or put makeup on my face. Instead, I do the exact opposite of society's norms. I usually have a crisp button-down broadcloth shirt with my hair tamed in a side part with pomade. Since the transition in my gender expression, having to perform a seemingly normal biological function is not as easy as it used to be.

While I never minded people committing the mistake of calling me "sir" or if sometimes they led me to the male dressing room section, it is a very different matter when I am inside a public restroom. I can't argue with people and correct them like I usually would when I am involved in political debates. Whenever I enter a public restroom, I am always reduced to what I look like and whether the things underneath all the clothing match the figure on the sign of the restroom door. It has already reached a point where I even dread using the public restroom unless I ask my female friends to accompany me inside to ease that uncomfortable feeling and to avoid getting the unnecessary corrections before I even enter.

On those very rare occasions when I really need to use one, I usually encounter one or both of the following scenarios: One, a staff member calls my attention and points me in the direction of the male restroom. Two, women entering the public restroom do a double take, unsure if they have entered the right restroom, usually with a confused look on their faces. While I know it is quite understandable why they can't quite wrap their head around the situation immediately, those confused looks cause me to feel a bit embarrassed about who I am and how I present myself even if no one has really told me to get out of the public restroom just yet.

Perhaps the most uncomfortable public restroom experience I had to endure was during my visit to Dumaguete. Drinking at a bar with a few of my friends one night, I excused myself to go to the restroom. I waited outside the female restroom and was told by a staff member that the male restroom was on the other side. I calmly pointed out to him that I was female and was waiting in line at the correct restroom. And while I knew I was a bit drunk that night after downing a few glasses of rum cola a few moments before, I still heard him say *"tomboy diay to"* (it was a lesbian) to his colleague. I guess I was fortunate to have been a little drunk as it helped me shake off the feeling of slight embarrassment afterward.

I can still remember the hurt I felt upon hearing that seemingly harmless remark from a man who didn't know better.

And since that day, I started to abhor having to use public restrooms even more.

I do not want to repeatedly go through that chore of having to explain myself that I am in the right restroom and negate the unnecessary corrections. I hate the feeling of having to wait a long time inside a public restroom because I don't want to see the slightly judgmental and confused stares from other women that always make me uncomfortable.

And to be honest, it has crossed my mind that maybe I should switch to the male restroom if it would make things less awkward for me and everyone else. But then again, I do not identify as male; it would make me more uncomfortable, and doing so would certainly cause a commotion. So regardless of which public restroom I choose to use, I know that it is inevitable that with the way things are, there will always be awkward questions and stares from strangers.

Because of this, whenever I do go out, I usually hope that the establishment I'll be visiting has a gender-neutral public restroom to obviate all the unnecessary questioning and awkwardness. Or else, I usually just go to the bathroom before I leave home or work. If left without any choice, I am forced to just suck it up and endure all the questions and confused stares again as if it were already part of my habit.

While we are currently living in times where there is relatively more awareness and acceptance about the existence of the LGBTQ community and their issues, some countries are struggling to keep up with the times. In countries like the Philippines, there is only tolerance, not acceptance, for LGBTQs.

While there has been relatively more representation of Filipino LGBTQs in the mainstream media compared to previous decades, we continue to face discrimination even for the most basic things—even things as simple as using the bathroom of our choice.

But I know that I live in relatively better circumstances compared to other Filipino LGBTQs. I am currently based in the nation's capital city where, most of the time, people couldn't care less about your life choices. I work in a university filled with critical-thinking minds, where no one really cares about how I express myself. I am judged and respected by my colleagues and superiors based on my ability to deliver and follow through.

If I did not have a career path that was noble and distinguished like a science career, I think most people wouldn't be giving me respect. Even to this day, it keeps me thinking, had the people I interacted with not known that I was a scientist, would they still treat me the same? Probably not.

I feel that because of the Filipino stereotype that LGBTQ people are only good for comic relief, most people would subscribe to this hasty generalization. Which is why for Filipino LGBTQ people, as compared to our heterosexual counterparts, there is more pressure to become "accomplished," or you should possess some sort of talent for show business so that you could become "acceptable" based on society's standards. While I do not criticize the LGBTQs who have careers in the said business, I do think that today's Filipino LGBTQs are so much more than what people see in the mainstream media—we are also writers, artists, lawyers, teachers, doctors, scientists, and so much more.

But even if we do pass this "acceptability" standard that is unfairly set forth upon us by society, every single day, Philippine social reality gives us a reality check: at least for now, the ceiling can only go up as high as tolerance.

I remember coming home on the weekends during my college days. Since my parents are quite religious, the whole family had to go to mass every Sunday. And on a few of those Sundays, I also remember sitting through the priest's homilies that criticized LGBTQs. Instead of spreading love and acceptance, some members of the church spread and perpetuate this toxic idea of LGBTQs living a life of sin.

And because religion is very much at the core of Filipino culture, it is quite difficult for the majority of Filipinos to unlearn this toxic and harmful notion of the LGBTQ community.

You and I know what the stereotypical bigot sounds like—they openly criticize LGBTQs for "living a life of sin" that goes against nature, depicting us as a result of a genetic error or as if we made a decision that could be overturned. It's also often difficult to detect if a person is exhibiting a subtle form of bigotry, especially from someone who is close to you.

I've experienced both explicit and subtle bigotry in various forms. But perhaps one experience that struck me the most was with an old friend. We had one of those low-maintenance friendships where you could pick up right where you left off. In one of our conversations, we talked about how she was preparing for her upcoming wedding, and naturally, I was invited to attend the ceremony. All was well and good until I heard this weird and unsettling request of hers: since I was a friend from childhood, maybe for old times' sake, I could wear a dress and be one of her bridesmaids.

While I valued our friendship, it was a request that I had to turn down as it went against who I am as a person. It may seem harmless, or maybe it was just an honest mistake on her part, but the thought of asking me to dress as someone that I am not—even for a single day—is painful, because it was like telling me that I should hide who I am from the rest of the world, or that she was ashamed of who I am. And while I did not make a big deal out of that weird request, it pained me to hear it from someone who I thought would have understood how I felt.

These subtle forms of bigotry could also be seen in phrases, whether explicit or implied, in words or in action: "I respect the LGBTQ community, but I don't think it's right for them to get married" or "You're different from the rest of them." And it is often that these subtle forms hurt us more than the explicit ones because they often come from someone familiar.

But despite the struggles we face every single day, I believe that we live in a time where people are still slowly learning to accept the LGBTQ community, and having the courage to live as an out and proud member is a deviant, nay, a revolutionary act, and is a contribution to the continuing struggle of gender equality all around the world. And for those of us who are brave enough to live out in the open, it is up to us to give a voice to the others who cannot live out in the open just yet. It is upon us to deepen people's understanding of sexual orientation and gender identity and expression to build a better society.

While it might seem that it is still impossible to attain acceptance in this generation's lifetime, all hope for a better future should not be lost to fear and doubt. It is better to contribute to this protracted struggle for acceptance and equality than to not have struggled at all.

Living life as a Filipino LGBTQ is quite similar to what I experience every time I go inside a public restroom. It's either you decide to hold everything in or you just do as you please and not give a damn about what everyone else thinks. Either way, whatever you choose to do, most people are still going to give you the same confused and judgmental looks.

Rough Like Velvet:
My Year in Guangzhou

By Colum Murphy

"**M**U Kelun. Why you not married?" asked the girl from Benin who was sitting at the top of the class. Peering out from under her beige knit cap, she continued: "Why you have no children?"

I was Mu Kelun, or at least that was my new Chinese name. It meant something to do with envy and Napoleon, and was given to me by a friend's father, a Singaporean Chinese man who studied calligraphy. Some of my friends thought it appropriate, scholarly, and suitable for a writer. Others found it pretentious.

Still, in China I've found it's useful to have a Chinese name. It's my plea to Chinese people to take me seriously. I'm a white, middle-aged man who is cuddly around the middle, and young people often see me as affable, benevolent—to be respected, sure, but from a safe distance, like an aging relative showing signs of dementia.

On that first day of class, especially, I felt like an elderly next-of-kin as I stood at the front of a sparsely decorated classroom filled with tiny wooden desks and chairs, crammed with about a dozen young men and women from around the world.

I was an incoming student at the Mandarin-for-foreigners program at Sun Yat-sen University in the southern Chinese city of Guangzhou. Named after the prominent revolutionary considered to be the founder of modern China, the university is one of China's most prestigious.

The selection process for foreigners to enter its Mandarin program is, however, not stringent at all. Not surprising then, studying Chinese there is especially popular among young people, particularly from developing nations. It offers them a legitimate way to come to the country, where they can also work on the side to earn a quick buck by sourcing goods manufactured in China to sell in their home countries.

I, on the other hand, had not come on an import–export run. I had not come for a job at all. In fact, I had given up my post in Hong Kong—I can't say cushy, because it wasn't, and I can't say reluctantly, because I hated it—to come live in mainland China. Why? The short answer was I came here for love. But I was damned if I was going to come to Guangzhou only for a relationship. So, I enrolled in a year-long Chinese course, where I would have to explain myself anew, this time to a motley cohort of language students.

When I introduced myself to them, I gave just the bare details needed to get through the ordeal.

Name: Mu Kelun.

Age: Forty-one.

Nationality: Irish.

Profession: Former journalist.

Reason for studying Mandarin in Guangzhou: To kill time

and make myself feel I am not wasting a year of my life chasing the love of an Indian Singaporean named Mohan.

(I kept the last thought to myself.)

*

Tall with long arms, Mohan sported a beard he jokingly described as "Taliban Chic." His big smile and self-deprecating humor tinged with an Aussie accent he acquired while he was a university student in Canberra made him immediately likeable. If he were not gay, Mohan would have been snapped up long ago by some beauty from the Sindhi community, the ethnic group of Indians to which he belonged.

Mohan had moved to Guangzhou from Singapore three years earlier. Like many Sindhis before him, he'd come to make his fortune as an export merchant based in China. But the timing wasn't right. As the country's economy flourished, costs were increasing, and profit margins were increasingly thin. The economic downturn sweeping the United States and other countries in the wake of the 2008 financial crisis didn't help.

I was never one to give up anything for anyone. I had earned the reputation of being a career-driven narcissist—not least in my own head. Before Mohan, I'd only ever held down one long-term relationship. That was with a doe-eyed young Spanish woman I'd met at university in Ireland. We were together for almost a decade, but inevitably, after all that time, we broke up.

The rest of my relationships had been with men, and

almost all of them short-term. They'd start out well. But it wouldn't be too long before I became bored, either with them, or my job, or my location. I was always on the lookout for the latest shiny new thing, the more exciting city, the more challenging job. I never gave too much thought to personal relations.

So it was out of character for me to up and leave a life of seven years in Hong Kong for a man in China. It wasn't such a sacrifice. My job at a shipping newspaper in Hong Kong had not worked out as planned. Leaving Hong Kong might help, I thought. Learning Chinese and delving into more literary forms of writing—and away from journalism—would be also a boon. It seemed moving to be with Mohan was the right thing to do.

I packed my belongings in Hong Kong, putting half in storage as a hedge for something going wrong. It was a short distance, but the move filled me with dread. From my comfortable perch in the former British colony, mainland China was a chaotic place that did not have rule of law, where dangers lurked at every corner—bus crashes, train collisions, nightclubs that caught fire, and where hospitals were ill-equipped and staffed by poorly trained doctors.

It was dark outside when we crossed into China near Shenzhen just past midnight on that September night in 2011—only an occasional red neon sign from some border-town love hotel to be seen. The air was hazy with pollution, obscuring the scenery from inside our rental minivan even more. Mohan took my hand and looked me in the eyes. "Don't worry, Murph," he said, using his favorite term of endearment for me. "It'll be all right."

*

Beijing has the ancient Forbidden City, the imposing Tian-
anmen Square and the Great Wall not too far away. Shanghai has the Bund, the skyscrapers of Pudong, and the quaint
streets of the former French Concession. But Guangzhou has
little by way of international acclaim. The twisting, pin-like
Guangzhou Tower is hardly world renowned, although China's largest trade show, the China Import and Export Fair,
or the Canton Fair, is familiar to some foreigners. Among
Chinese, Guangzhou is known as one of the country's top
culinary hubs. Even so, the city of more than fourteen million
is a pale shadow of bustling, cosmopolitan—even at half the
size—Hong Kong, less than 200 kilometers to the south.

Guangzhou is a kind of tale of three cities: Canton,
Guangzhou, and Gwangjau. Three variations of the same
name for the same place in three different languages, the con
notations of each almost suggesting three separate cities.

In colonial times, the British referred to this place as Canton. It's a name that, for some, is exotic, conjuring up an era
when city served as a powerful hub for global trade that was
dominated by foreigners. But Canton was far from idyllic. In
The Opium War: Drugs, Dreams and the Making of China, writer Julia Lovell states that Lord Auckland, a former governor
of India, once described Canton as "perhaps the least pleasant
residence for a European on the face of the earth."

Then there's Guangzhou, the city's name in Mandarin,

the official language of the People's Republic of China. This Guangzhou is modern China's third largest city, with millions of its residents hailing from other parts of China. While this group includes highly educated Chinese in pursuit of professional opportunities, it also includes other Chinese "migrant workers," who leave their hometowns and villages to come to the city to work in lower-paying jobs such as security guard, restaurant wait staff, or masseuse. For many migrants, Guangzhou will never be their true home. They are considered just fleeting visitors by the city whose true name is Gwangjau, its local, Cantonese name.

Though connected by Cantonese, Hong Kong and Guangzhou are like estranged siblings, living completely different lives. Hong Kong is built on finance, banking, and law—a city where executives in sharp suits and neat shirts and ties meet in plush air-conditioned conference rooms overlooking Victoria Harbor, plotting their next multibillion-dollar takeovers or stock-exchange listings. Guangzhou has little of that glamour. It's a sprawling metropolis through which flows the Pearl River. For long, it secured much of its income by selling low-cost, low-quality consumer goods in global markets including large foreign retailers such as Wal-Mart. It's not an ugly city, and as China develops, so too does Guangzhou: the city is now home to some inspiring examples of contemporary architecture, including the Opera House, designed by Iraqi-British architect Zaha Hadid. Still, despite such glimmers of the future, when I lived there, the gap between that city and its southern neighbor Hong Kong was pronounced, and Guangzhou still had that hard-core, haphazard, slightly unnerving feel of a place where anything could—and frequently did—happen.

During my time there, I used to take the bus from my high-rise apartment in the Yuexiu District and cross the Pearl River to the Haizhu District to the south and to the sprawling green Sun Yat-sen University campus. Sometimes I would close my eyes and convince myself that the Pearl River was in fact the Seine, and that I was living the writer's life, like James Baldwin and countless others, in "Gay Paree."

Then I'd wake up. Usually because the bus driver had just swerved violently to avoid yet another unsupervised toddler, or simply because I'd reached my stop. I realized that even if the semi-permanent polluted haze hanging overhead was photoshopped out, "GZ"—as some of my cool classmates liked to call it—was no Paris, and, was not outwardly gay in the least.

*

"Mu Kelun. Why you not married? Why you have no children? I can't figure you out."

Yueliang, the stylish young African girl's Chinese name, means "moon." One of the first words of Chinese she learned was *jiatofa*—the word for wig. The color and style of her hair changed almost daily, morphing from Beyoncé one day to Rihanna the next, to Sade the following, before returning to Beyoncé. She was one of three girls from Benin in my class, all related. These African girls' parents pushed them to come to China to learn its language in anticipation of closer business ties between China and Africa.

Guangzhou is home to China's largest African population. It's difficult to put a precise number on how many Africans live here since many are not permanent residents. Some estimate more than 200,000 people from Africa live in the city. Many just come for short periods—two, three months—before returning to Africa with suitcases loaded with samples of items such as clothes, belts, and jewelry. Once they strike deals with merchants back home, they arrange shipments in containers that set sail from China stuffed with merchandise, bound for the markets of Luanda and Lagos, Addis Ababa and Abidjan.

Yueliang dominated the Beninese trio. She sat right up front and was the class prefect, running for chalk when supplies ran out and telling off other students for talking in class. She was also determined to "figure me out."

I tried to evade her probing questions with coyness. "*Bu gaosu ni*," I replied. This, according to our teacher, Ms. Chen, was a polite way of saying "buzz off" in Chinese. It didn't really work. Yueliang just played with a strand of her hair, glanced sideways at the other students, and said: "*Mu Kelun hen qiguai*." "Mu Kelun, you're weird."

It was if I were back in a classroom when I was twelve or thirteen in Ireland, when I used to be called things much worse than "weird"—names like "sissy," "girly," "gay," and "fag." I thought I had come a long way since then, but here I was again, at the front of a classroom, looking at the faces of my new classmates, trying to decide whether I should come out to them. *Will I? Won't I?*

People rarely openly say, "I hate gays"—although perhaps in places like Russia or Uganda and a host of other countries, such vitriol is all too common. Instead, it's insidious. Like someone saying, "That's so gay," or singing a rap song with lyrics that say, "No homo" within earshot. They may not intend to antagonize a specific person, but their words serve to exclude, reminding any gay person present that the world is still very much a straight one.

Some months later, the topic of being gay came up again during one of many class digressions on dating. Mali, the Colombian girl with the classic looks of a typical Miss Colombia who came to China to buy handbags and accessories to sell in her native Medellin, put up her hand to ask the teacher a question.

"Teacher Chen. What's the Chinese word for 'gay'?" she asked. Ms. Chen was rarely fazed by students' questions. But this time she seemed flustered. She grimaced, her face tight with disgust. "Mali. *Bu xing!*" she said, making clear her displeasure at the question and declining to answer.

But Mali really wanted to know. The class erupted in collective, nervous laughter. I put up my hand. "Teacher Chen, I know," I said, my voice trembling a little. "It's *tongzhi.*"

The room fell silent. I imagined the youngsters connecting dots in their heads. The teacher wrote the word on the blackboard, adding it to a list of new vocabulary we had learned that morning. She resumed her normal teaching pose and began to explain how it originally had meant "comrade" but had since been corrupted by "those Hong Kong people" and how the word now was commonly used to mean homosexual.

Once Ms. Chen had finished her explanation of the two characters, she erased them swiftly from the board, leaving the other words from our vocabulary list untouched. "*Bu hao! Bu hao!*" she said aloud, shaking her head. "No good! No good!"

*

The first time I spotted Mohan was in Guangzhou around three years before finally I moved there to be with him. I was in the city on a reporting assignment with a straight colleague. After we'd filed our stories, I persuaded him to accompany me for a drink at Velvet, a gay bar and club I'd found online.

From the outside it looked innocuous—with only a small sign with an etching of a Menorah-like candleholder calling attention to the doorway. Once we passed the blue curtains—made from velvet of course—the first thing that struck me was the huge, rectangular bar, the far end of which was a glass-covered platform that doubled as a stage for erotic dancers. It was a relatively quiet midweek night. Entertainment was courtesy of two tanned muscular Brazilian men wearing only Doc Martens boots and tight cotton briefs, on the back of which was written in ALL CAPS the word "ITALIA."

"Another beer?" my colleague asked, trying to maintain studied indifference. I didn't answer. I had taken my eyes off the dancers just long enough to notice a lanky Indian with orange-framed glasses who had just entered. Not bad, I thought, as I turned my gaze back to the two ITALIAs and our two beer bottles, which at this point were vibrating, too, and were teetering toward the edge of the bar.

Two nights later, with my colleague safely dispatched back to Hong Kong, I headed out on the town alone, directing myself this time to a different gay venue. For a city with such a large population, the city's gay scene was small. It wasn't long before I bumped into the bearded Indian again.

The venue was crowded that night, full of revelers who'd come to celebrate the arrival of summer. Despite the buzzing crowd, we managed to hold a conversation. I tried to impress him with my knowledge of the Indian diaspora. Twelve years younger than me, Mohan was intelligent, funny, and handsome with his easy, broad smile. But it wasn't until a few weeks later when he happened to be in Hong Kong for a visit that finally we got together, our intimacy expedited by more than a few happy-hour cocktails. That encounter would set the stage for what would become my first serious gay relationship—one that would see me uprooting my comfortable Hong Kong life, leading me to Guangzhou and, eventually, an extended connection with mainland China.

At the start of our relationship, Mohan would come down to Hong Kong to see me on weekends. Once, on a whim, he traveled for dinner midweek—a total investment of around six hours, travel time included. Occasionally, I would go see him in Guangzhou. As a working journalist, getting even a tourist visa to China could be problematic, and so it was often more convenient for him to visit me. Eventually, the to and fro became tedious, and we began to look for a more permanent solution. I decided that meant moving to Guangzhou—the place we first met.

My move to be with Mohan—and maybe my move away

from everything comfortable and familiar about my life—
would be the trigger that finally pushed me to come out to
my own family. But unlike Mohan, who was lucky in some
ways to have been able to come out to his mother despite the
conservative Sindhi culture, I had lost my chance with mine.

The Ireland of my childhood in the 1970s was not exactly
liberal. For the most part, the Roman Catholic Church was
in firm control of the country's education system and exerted
strong influence over national dialogue in the country's media. In the poverty and ignorance of my parents' generation,
conservative values flourished. Openly gay men and women
were extremely rare. My parents were also devout Catholics.
My father, who worked in the kitchens at a local airport, was
always too busy making a living to cast judgment on others.
His life was work and prayer before he succumbed to cancer
when I was around sixteen. My mother kept more a watchful
eye on her children, maintaining a firm grip to make sure we
didn't wander too far from the "right" track.

I waited until I was in a gay relationship, until Mohan,
to start coming out to my family. By that time, I was almost
forty, and my mother had already died. I still wonder whether
I did the right thing by never sharing my true self with her.

*

The best time to arrive at Velvet was just after midnight, when
the customers inside were well on their way to getting high
and the dancers were gyrating in full swing. Those days, it was
usually Penny who performed. Chinese with long blond hair,

she liked to thrust about in a black bikini made from shiny fake leather.

At its busiest, male customers would line up three rows deep parallel to the bar as if in a choir. They were mainly Chinese and nearly all in their early twenties. Most were shorter than me, and I am not particularly tall. They also were slimmer. I used to be slim—two decades earlier when I was their age. Nearly all of them smoked.

Some of the foreign clientele were traders from Egypt, Lebanon, Colombia, and Russia in town for business or the Canton Fair. They stumbled into Velvet, some by mistake, or so they said. (Velvet didn't openly bill itself as gay.)

The local clientele was a mixed bunch. Many of the young Chinese who came here preferred to use their English names that were given to them when they were younger by perhaps an English teacher, or that they invented themselves. There was Eros who said he worked "in media," Eagle the modern dancer, and Coco the student.

One night I watched two Chinese boys make out in a corner. It was almost like an anthropological documentary on the National Geographic channel. They groped each other inexpertly; their lips rubbed together in a circular motion, their bodies at an awkward distance. It looked as if they were kissing through a glass pane. Still, I was happy to see them in blatant defiance of the silly "No Kissing" sign that hung just a couple of feet away from their bobbing heads.

Most of us came to forget our real selves. To dance, to flirt, to be with friends, maybe to get lucky. We didn't want to be reminded of who we were or the pressures on the outside, past the velvet curtains.

For some, that meant the prying parents who wanted to know when they would get married—as inevitably many did. For others, it was a chance to avoid overly curious co-workers or college classmates, with their persistent questions or homophobic jokes.

Life in the new city with Mohan was exciting, but less ideal than we'd hoped. A string of deals that had gone bad began to put Mohan on edge. I tried to pretend everything was fine, offering advice on how he might reverse his fortunes. But it was of little use. My counsel wasn't enough to stem the reality that his business was in trouble. Around the time I had relocated to Guangzhou, Mohan's mother had also decided to move to the city from her native Singapore so she could keep an eye on her son, his business, and his increasingly troubling health issues caused mainly from overwork or stress. Though she never outright said it, it was clear she would never accept the two of us living together. I rented an apartment across town from Mohan and his mother. We'd meet up for meals or outings almost daily. But it was like a series of dates, akin to when we were living in different cities. I looked for ways to fill my time, with study and writing. One night when I went to Velvet with a friend, egged on by too much beer, I flirted with a visiting Ukrainian. As time drew on, there would be other occasions when I would stray even further.

*

Often, when class finished, some of my classmates would cast their textbooks aside and head to Xiao Bei Lu—or Small North Road—Guangzhou's main African neighborhood, in search of fun and a bit of pampering and a taste of home. The street brimmed with people. Chinese Muslim women in beaded hijabs cooked chicken on makeshift grills, the smell of charcoal wafting through the air. African women strolled to salons to get their nails painted or hair braided. African men, hunched in small groups, drank beer and bantered. Children—African, Chinese, and mixed—darted around, calling out in Chinese. Now and then a Middle Eastern or Indian face would appear. There were only a few Caucasians.

Down the street, the Elephant Trade Mall was popular with Africans. Each floor was jammed with small units, where African entrepreneurs set up boutiques, barber shops, hair salons, and restaurants. Chez Roba, on the fourth floor, was a haven for Congolese craving bites from their motherland. A peek into stainless steel chafing dishes revealed the day's menu: goat, beans, and *fufu*, a starchy staple made from vegetables.

At night, animated diners swilled beers, speaking loudly in a mixture of French and Lingala—the language found in the Democratic Republic of the Congo. In the background, music videos showed men and women dancing in formation, shaking their hips seductively to the strains of a *soukous* dance number, the kind that's popular in parts of Africa.

Many of my classmates went back to Africa for spring break, and given Mohan's busy schedule, his mother's presence, and simply because I had the time and money to do so, I found myself also booking a ticket to the continent. I also had a goal, since I, too, had family in Africa. My older brother had lived in Malawi for close to two decades, and I was finally ready to come out to him.

Eugene had gone to Africa decades earlier, first to Tanzania, then Mozambique, before finally settling in Malawi. A trained car mechanic, he had built a life with his British wife and four sons and was running his own successful auto-repair business. Physically we were worlds apart. I had a shock of curly red hair, slightly bucked teeth, and freckles—lots of freckles. His complexion was darker, even Mediterranean. As a child, he was a gifted sportsman. I spent hours at the public library, browsing travel books on China and Russia.

One early memory I have is of Eugene and his prized possession—a red and white Honda 50 motorbike. Once, when I was around eight, he lifted me up and gently placed me on the front of the saddle. I sat there, wedged between his arms, his body acting as a kind of armor. Buildings whisked by as we sped around our housing estate. I watched the speedometer edge its way up. The engine hummed quietly as the wind flicked my hair to one side then back again. I laughed. The bike glided smoothly even as my brother skillfully maneuvered to avoid potholes. When we pulled up outside our house, Eugene set me down, then his bike roared off into the horizon.

The distance between us increased over the decades as we lived at opposite ends of the world. I hoped my visit to Africa would bring us closer.

Approaching the end of my three-week spring break in Malawi, I finally got a chance to be alone with him for the first time since I arrived. "Will you have a whiskey?" Eugene offered. "Sure," I replied.

I rarely drank whiskey, but the expensive bottle I picked up in Johannesburg airport duty-free store was going down remarkably well. I watched him as he scooped two large cubes of ice into a crystal tumbler. He opened the bottle and didn't stop pouring until the golden liquid covered the ice. We chatted about the day gone by and the plans for the next.

The whiskey, my gift to him, could open doors, open things, open people—as if magically. It seemed to be working on Eugene that night. He began to recount some of the difficulties he'd faced raising teenage boys in a country that was not, ultimately, their own.

All I could think of was getting the reason why I'd come to Africa for off my chest. But first I would give my brother the stage, allow him time to talk through what was on his mind. After our third drink, we retired for the night. I thought it best not to push too much.

By the following morning I had resolved to make sure there was no ambiguity in my brother's mind about how I was living my life. I suppose I wanted him to ask: *Do you have a partner? Is he a good person? What is he like? Are you happy?* That didn't happen. A couple of times, just when I thought the conversation was heading in the right direction, someone or something would interrupt. Now time was running out.

A few evenings later, I found Eugene again in the living room, sitting in his favorite armchair. "Do you want to watch this?" I said, holding a DVD in my hand. "It's from my last trip to Ireland."

I had visited Ireland a few months earlier and Mohan had joined me. The DVD contained video shots and photos of us together. The images loaded and were displayed on the television screen, accompanied by a ragtime soundtrack. They continued to appear one after the other. Yet, still, neither of us had said a word about the bearded Indian character. No acknowledgment. No tacit nod. Nothing. It was as if this Indian man on the screen were a stranger, a passerby, who had accidentally wandered into camera range. But I knew he wasn't just anybody. He was Mohan.

I knew if I said nothing, I would be complicit in denying Mohan's existence, and my own. It would have meant that I had come to Africa for nothing.

"Oh! That's Mohan!" I said casually. "Have you heard about him?" Eugene shook his head. "He's my partner," I said, my voice slightly trembling mid-sentence. An awkward silence followed, but I didn't care. I had said what I'd come to say.

A few days later, when I was leaving for Guangzhou, Eugene left me with some parting words. He advised me not to let a relationship get in the way of my career. He didn't mention Mohan by name, but I knew who he meant.

*

Around one month after I got back from Africa, I received a job offer to return to journalism as a reporter in the Shanghai bureau of a prominent American business newspaper. I hesitated at first, thinking what the move might mean for my relationship, and contemplated what giving up my life in Guangzhou might entail. By that time I'd made more friends, and my time in the city had begun to yield results. My Chinese had improved; I'd got to do some writing; I'd even found the time and courage to come out to my brother—all of this would not have been possible were it not for my Guangzhou sojourn. Still, I wasn't in love with the city, and I was increasingly not sure about where I stood with Mohan. At the back of my mind, my brother's parting words rang clear. I took the job and moved to Shanghai.

When I look back on that period in Guangzhou, I'm grateful for it—the year gave me the space and distance to come to terms with who I was a person.

Those irritating questions from my classmates got under my skin because I wasn't comfortable in it. By disconnecting with what was familiar and secure in Hong Kong—a well-paid career at a global media brand, an extensive network of friends—and trading that for rather isolated existence in a high-rise overlooking the sprawl of Guangzhou and its transitory dwellers from Africa and from around China, I'd departed from everything that I knew. Even my frustrations with Mohan helped shape me into the person I am today. My time with him there showed me possibilities of what a gay relationship, or even a marriage, might or could look like. In my case, that picture of relationship bliss doesn't include him, although we remain in touch. I didn't end up writing a China novel or a work of nonfiction that captured the essence of Guangzhou, but I did have experiences and developed deep relationships that have helped nurture the writer in me.

I've lost touch with most of my classmates, apart from occasional sightings on Facebook. The girls have gone back to Benin. Photos of Mali affecting various poses from sites around Colombia suggest she's also returned home. Mohan and his mother eventually relocated to Singapore. In Shanghai, I would later meet Jiawei, now my boyfriend. We're planning to get married. I'm writing more, but perhaps not as regularly as I would like.

I only occasionally return to Guangzhou. On one such occasion, I went back to where Velvet used to be. Penny, the Brazilians, the "No Kissing" sign were all gone. Velvet was gone, and in its place was a straight bar.

Note: Some names have been changed.

IN DEFENCE OF DYKE SHIRTS (AND MARRIAGE EQUALITY)

By Jenna Collett

MY girlfriend has a glitzy media job.
And by that I mean they work her into the ground, but the perks mean she's grateful for the soil between her teeth. Her work gets her close enough to smell the sweat of the hospitality industry in Hong Kong, and occasionally she gets to attend soirées, wine tastings, restaurant openings, yacht christenings, club closings, the re-opening of a re-release on a foreclosed dream.

Tonight is a club opening: a bare knuckled, three-finger-deep into the canapés, post-free-wine pre-free-cocaine-if-you-know-the-owner brawl, with hors d'oeuvres touted by careening servers who will duck, weave, and wave if they don't know you—and they don't know you, Felicia.

I don't like these parties, but I also know I should like these parties. The third time I get duck-weaved and waved I shout, "I can buy my own food you know," and the server looks back at me as if to say, "But this food, though?"

Tonight we can't stop the servers for love nor casual flirtation. People are diving in front of them like they are trying to take a stiletto between the ribs for an insurance claim. But these are battle-hardened waitrons who could side-step you so efficiently that when you look up they are nowhere, and you are getting shark-smiled at by an older man at the bar, wondering how his wedding-banded hand comes to be anywhere near the small of your back.

We'd both just got off work and the game plan was to eat before we got into the opening celebration's free-flow wine and cocktails. But we'd already sunk two gins as we watched the food go by, and the plan was unravelling fast.

Others are having a similar issue, and tongues start to loosen as empty bellies fill with booze. As I hover at the kitchen door in an attempt at a better strategy, I find myself in conversation with a Suit who needs the advice of a stranger. Which is to say: he needs advice he can freely ignore, or adopt—along with the credit.

"You see that girl over there? Sorry, *woman*. See that woman over there?"

"The one taking selfies with a selfie-light?"

"The same. Anyway, she's from Macau, been dating my friend for three months. My friend is French. Nice guy, real nice guy."

I nod along, lifting a feeble hand to try and stop a waiter who shot out of the saloon doors.

"She's already talking about marriage. Doesn't have a job. No job. Supposedly can't work because of visa issues. Anyway, my friend's a good-looking guy, good-looking French guy, you know, with permanent residency. In finance, you know. Good-looking guy. Nice guy. Do you know what I'm saying?"

"Maybe if you say it, I will."

"Don't you think three months is too short to be talking about getting married? And he's a nice French guy. *With money.*" He says the last sentence like it's italicised.

"I'd be more upset about the selfie-light thing."

"Well, that, too, but I'm mainly worried about my friend. He's already paying for everything. And he's too far in to see it. Do you think I should talk to him?"

"You know the answer to that. You can't talk to friends about their shitty SOs. With your luck, they'll get married and live happily ever after, and you'll be that guy at their wedding that said she was looking for PIN numbers. Bad idea."

"I know. But I still feel like I should do something."

"Does he drink?"

"Oh yeah. Why?"

"If you absolutely have to say something, get him drunk first. That way he probably won't remember you said anything."

He looks at me as if he'd picked the wrong stranger, and narrows his eyes at the good-looking Frenchman's girlfriend of three months.

"And she's wearing cut-offs in here, for fuck's sake."

*

I return to my girlfriend, defeated in my quest for unpaid-for food. From the left, a square of gorgeous shirt leans in: all muted purples and khakis, patterns hard to spot under the you-don't-really-want-to-see-this-place-anyway lighting. But it was without a doubt a Dyke Shirt, the kind you only used to see on lesbians in the eighties and nineties, but now see on hipster men who have kindly updated the style by slimming the fit and binning the block pastels and geometric shapes: a style now borrowed back with fervour by lesbians and trans men.

The Shirt says, "What food you want?"

"Ah, thanks, that's kind, don't worry about us, we're fine," we slur.

(We'll just sit here getting more fucked up than is appropriate on a Wednesday.)

"No, what food do you want?"

Sensing the power of the Shirt, and the pointed addition of grammar to the question, we indicate the canapés we like, which are floating by in the trajectory of an enraged bumblebee. The next time the Shirt lifts her hand, a maroon-vested server comes over before you can say, "Do we even say 'dyke' anymore?"

"Thanks," I say, "I like your shirt." The woman looks at me as if I'd told her the Earth was round and expected a cookie. She nods and goes back to her conversation at the next table. The interaction was over and we weren't required to repay her with anything, least of all an unimaginative compliment.

We gratefully eat our fill and start to sober up. Seeing as the canapés only come in minute servings of three at a time, though, encircled with smears of "reduction" (I've always wondered what it is that's been reduced), they quickly run out. Again the Shirt lifts a casual hand, and again the server promptly delivers.

*

There is a look women who have short hair give to other women with short hair. A tacit acknowledgement. But there are degrees of recognition in this look. If you happen to pass a straight woman with short hair, you still share the look, which is essentially just an interlocking of eye-contact that's much longer than your average appraisal of a stranger. There may even be that accompanying imperceptible nod that explains that you, too, have deviated. You, too, are different. But shortly after this moment, the straight woman will look away, indicating that this exchange can only go so far. Rather than homophobic, it feels humane. There are answers here. By contrast, if you pass a queer woman with short hair, there will be no looking away. Or rather, there will be a looking away, only to look back again. In this split-second's return there is real recognition. It is different from saying, "I, too, am deviant." Instead this look says, "I see you in the absence of deviance."

These interactions are often more likely to happen between queer women of a similar age range, or of similar cultural backgrounds. The addition of age and culture allows for doubt. Am I seeing who I think I'm seeing? Or is this the hairstyle, gait, or posturing associated with an age group, or cultural identity? Is your hair short because you're gay, or did you just love the nineties, Faye Wong in *Chungking Express*? Are you holding hands because you are lovers, or are we just in a part of the world where women hold hands?

*

Our Shirt was Filipino, strong-set, with short cropped hair.

She wore khaki slacks, an impressive leather belt, loafers, and, of course, the shirt. Her companion was also Filipino with long hair, dressed in a brightly coloured blouse. They were both older, but it's hard to tell how much. I guess forties, but find out later that they are in their early sixties and late fifties respectively. At the table next to ours they converse infrequently in low Tagalog: the report of two birds coming to sound at day's light.

My girlfriend, a woman who can hold her liquor but not her questions, thanks them again and asked how long they had been together.

There was a pause before… "Twenty-seven years" and then the look.

"How about you two?"

"Eleven years."

"Wow. Long time."

"Ha, it's not twenty-seven years."

"Eleven years is long enough." We all laugh, more recognition.

There are smiles, and I offer to get us all some wine.

"What is this wine anyway?"

"It's South African, where we're from," my girlfriend says. "Embarrassing, but it's pretty much all we drink here—because we know what to buy, and it's cheap." The Shirt mentions they prefer South American and Australian wines, finding French wine to be "kind of nothing." We agree excitedly, and not untruthfully, that New World wines have more of a kick, which we can all get behind.

More sips are taken. We find connections across age and

race, waving our flags as part of the Global South. It's important to make distinctions here; we are different from those that
mingle around us: French bankers, high-society Hongkongers,
the big money. Although we, being two English-speaking
white women, wave these flags far more fervently.

We talk more about wine, and where we're all from versus
where we've lived and worked. Hong Kong is home to these
two women, who've both been here around thirty years. It's
fairly new to us in comparison.

We stay clear of the topic that's usually voiced when the
length of our relationship is mentioned. It is largely inevitable that when a stranger, usually a heterosexual stranger, finds
out how long we have been together, the topic of marriage
is raised. Whether the related questions of why and how are
asked to showcase a progressive disposition, or out of clueless
curiosity, the tone often smacks of an onlooker at the zoo, asking after the mating habits of an unusually adorned bird. (The
answers are: for fun and for life, like everybody else.)

So, in the face of a relationship that began in 1990, and
the knowledge that marriage is not legal in the Philippines
nor in their adopted home, neither I nor my girlfriend plan on
asking any questions about marriage.

But there's been recent news that turns us toward the
topic: Taiwan had just made great strides toward legislation,
which we applaud for being the first country in Asia to do
so, and an expat woman who married her partner outside
Hong Kong was granted a visa usually reserved for heterosexual spouses (a case which the Shirt speculates will come
to naught for local Chinese). Australia was only beginning to

talk about a postal vote.

Instead, it was our new friends who brought up marriage in relation to us.

"Can you get married in South Africa?" the Shirt asks.

"Yeah, it's the only country on the continent where it's legal," we say. More tempering, more flag waving.

"But if you get married there and move to another country, they won't recognise it anyway, right?" the Blouse asks.

"Yes, unless that expat case we were talking about becomes more commonplace, but it's a country-to-country basis for sure."

"Ah Hong Kong will never: they're too afraid of immigrants. Unless they're here to clean and leave," the Blouse laughs.

They don't ask why my partner and I aren't married, despite us having the option to do so. And even though the question clings logically to the conversation, I don't expect it.

Glasses are topped up. More toasting. The music becomes louder and we have to raise our voices and lean in. There is a flush to our cheeks, the rouge heat of alcohol and the revelation of things held close to the chest, things only now and then exposed to the pink swirl of lights at a club. Answers to unspoken questions that usually come with caveats and cushioning; answers that are different in the daylight. Careful answers are made careless under the influence of all this red.

We learn that it took the better part of their relationship for the Blouse's family to accept them. That the family tried everything from threats to isolation, and that it took much convincing and time. Coming from the double-bind of a

Catholic Asian background, where relationships are premised on procreation and the provision of familial support, the Shirt had to take pains to assure the family that her partner would be taken care of. Years where—when they allowed themselves to look—the family began to see that there were no lengths she could not go to, no deficiency in the love she would give.

"They eventually understood that I will look after her," she says, still dogged in her promise.

There were also stories told of their life together. The normalcy of learning to be lovers and then family, of vacations, of an ashtray thrown in a particularly passionate fight, of three stitches above an eyebrow, bank statements and tax returns, night shifts and laundry, the daily housework of love.

We have our own stories, but stay quiet, grateful to see a future rarely reflected. We ask them every question besides, but they eventually get to it anyway.

"Twenty-seven years. No marriage." The phrases are uttered toughly. "Why would we get married? We can go to Cali and get married. We can go to Canada and get married. For what? For face? We'll get no recognition, no security, no property. I'm sixty-fucking-four. Why must I marry for face? I have a house. I've got a lawyer. The papers don't say married, but she gets my house. She'll get everything."

The word "face" is said with force, and I see a woman who has held on to hers, despite a life in which she was meant to lose a great deal.

We nod along vigorously. Of course, we understand. My girlfriend excuses herself to go to the bathroom. While she's gone, the Blouse takes a sip and asks me if we ever plan to get married.

"I'm going to ask her this year, but she doesn't know. Don't say anything."

Wine glasses clatter as they both clap their hands and their mouths open into joy, a flurry of promises not to tell spilling out, genuine pleasure on their faces.

"I just hope she doesn't say no," I quip to ease the tension in my heart. The moment is heavy with all our promised lives.

"She won't say no," the Blouse cries, her smile reassuring.

"No no," the Shirt nods resolutely, looking at her partner's face. "Never."

EDITORS

Carmen Ho

Carmen Ho is a Chinese–Canadian writer, editor, and fierce advocate of LGBTQ+ rights. She has an MFA in creative writing from City University of Hong Kong and a certificate in publishing from Ryerson University, Toronto. Her short story, "Seagull," is published in the anthology *Afterness: Literature from the New Transnational Asia* (After-Party Press, 2016). Carmen is currently working on her first novel, which she hopes will resonate with people who, like her, are queer and live in between cultures. She believes the literary landscape should be as beautiful and diverse as our collective humanity.

Gregg Schroeder

Gregg Schroeder is a writer and editor. He has co-edited print and online literary journals and anthologies, including *Afterness: Literature from the New Transnational Asia* (After-Party Press, 2016). His creative work has appeared in *The New Guard* and *Blood and Thunder*. Gregg earned his MFA in fiction from City University of Hong Kong and his undergraduate degree in journalism from Cal Poly San Luis Obispo in California. He is the coordinator of the Tongzhi Literary Group, promoting LGBT+ writing in Hong Kong. He has been working on a novel for a long, long time.

CONTRIBUTORS

Aaron Chan

Aaron Chan was born in Vancouver, British Columbia, and is a musician, filmmaker, and writer. He has a diploma in Screenwriting from Vancouver Film School and a BFA in Creative Writing from the University of British Columbia. His writing has been published in various literary magazines including *Wilde*, *Ricepaper*, *Existere*, *Plenitude, filling station,* and *Polychrome Ink*. His memoir piece, "A Case of Jeff," won *subTerrain*'s Lush Triumphant Literary Award in 2013. Aaron's debut book, *This City Is a Minefield*, a collection of memoir and personal essays, will be published in 2019 by Signal 8 Press. His website is www.theaaronchan.com and he tweets at @theaaronchan.

Jenna Collett

Jenna Collett is a South African lecturer living and working in Hong Kong. She knows less about finance than fiction, and more about sonnets than skyscrapers, but please don't quiz her on any of it. She has lived in South Africa, South Korea, and South China, and hopes always to reside in and write from the South of Somewhere.

Nancy L. Conyers

Nancy L. Conyers's stories and essays have been published in *Tiferet, Alluvium, The Citron Review, Lunch Ticket, The Manifest-Station, NüVoices*, and *Role Reboot*. She contributed the last chapter to *Unconditional: A Guide to Loving and Supporting Your LGBTQ Child*. She holds an MFA in Creative Writing from Antioch University in Los Angeles and is currently enrolled in the novel-writing certificate program at Stanford. Nancy has been an official and unofficial trailing spouse in Shanghai, Hong Kong, Italy, Sweden, and Singapore. Her website is www.nancylconyers.com.

Edward Gunawan

Edward Gunawan is a writer and filmmaker from Indonesia. He is a producer of two award-winning feature films that were both selected as Thailand's entry to the Best Foreign Language Film category for the Academy Awards. Currently co-writing the sci-fi studio film adaptation of Hao Jingfang's Hugo Award-winning novella *Folding Beijing*, Edward also actively promotes mental-health wellness through a volunteer online community that he founded: Project Press Play. His projects and blog can be found at www.addword.com.

Huang Haisu

Huang Haisu writes about Chinese people whose lives have been radically altered via connections with the international community. Her works in numerous publications include *The Letters Page* in the UK, *Sixth Tone* in mainland China, and Liars' League Hong Kong. She is a graduate of the former MFA program in Creative Writing at City University of Hong Kong. Her essay on the program's closure is published in *Afterness: Literature from the New Transnational Asia* (After-Party Press, 2016). In addition to her writing, Haisu is a full-time PhD student and a graduate employee of the Sociology Department at the University of Oregon in the United States.

Hayley Katzen

Hayley Katzen lives with her partner on a cattle farm in the Australian bush. Her first major publication was a textbook on Administrative Law. Since then, she has written and produced a play, *Pressure Point*, and her short stories have been produced for radio and published in Australian and American journals and anthologies including *Award Winning Australian Writing*. Her essays too have won awards and been published in Australian and American journals including *Australian Book Review*, *Griffith Review*, *Southerly*, *Fourth Genre*, and *Kenyon Review*. She has an MFA from City University of Hong Kong, and has recently completed a memoir.

Germaine Trittle P. Leonin

Germaine Trittle P. Leonin was educated at the University of the Philippines where she took up a Bachelor of Science in Agribusiness Management, a Bachelor of Laws, and a Master of Arts in English Studies, majoring in Creative Writing. While she is proficient in technical writing and legalese, she tries to do literary and feature writing whenever she can. Her talent has been especially useful in her day-job as well as her

LGBT-rights advocacy. She is a founding member of several Filipino LGBT organizations including her own Promoting Rights and Equality for Society's Marginalized (PRISM) and an all-women writers' group, Women in Bliss.

Krista V. Melgarejo

Krista V. Melgarejo always knew that she had an affinity for science, writing, and the ocean. She is an opinion columnist for *Squeeze PH* and is a contributor for *The Xylom*. She believes that writing and art are the best therapies for the soul. Born and raised in Davao City, Philippines, she is currently working as a science researcher and is finishing her graduate degree in marine science at the University of the Philippines Diliman.

Colum Murphy

Colum Murphy is an Irish journalist and writer based in Shanghai. He is the founder of Chinarrative.com, a website and newsletter that showcases the best in nonfiction writing from and about China. Until recently, he was the nonfiction editor of *The Shanghai Literary Review*. Murphy holds an MFA in Creative Nonfiction Writing from City University of Hong Kong.

Ingvild Solvang

Ingvild Solvang is from the Arctic island Andøya in Norway. An anthropologist and international development professional, she has worked globally for twenty years primarily based in Asia including Indonesia, Timor-Leste, and Seoul, South

Korea, where she currently lives with her partner and two daughters. She has an MFA in Creative Writing from City University of Hong Kong. She is fascinated by cultures, religions, and human contradictions and can't imagine a sadder condition than closed-mindedness.

Ember Swift

Canadian artist Ember Swift is a writer and musician living in Beijing. A columnist for several local magazines, her blog, "Queer Girl Gets Married," won the 2013 Lotus Blossom "Best Love Blog" award. Ember is seeking to publish her completed memoir, excerpts of which can be found in: *Asia Literary Review* (winter 2016); *Knocked Up Abroad: Stories of Pregnancy, Birth, and Raising a Family in a Foreign Country* (Amazon, 2016); and *How Does One Dress to Buy Dragonfruit: True Stories of Expat Women in Asia* (Signal 8 Press, 2014). Musically, Ember has released twelve albums of original music and performs regularly internationally. Her website is www.emberswift.com.

Agatha Verdadero

Agatha Verdadero wants her profile to highlight what she wants to be known and remembered for: that her identity is wrapped up, foremost, in her personal relationship with God. It's been often a messy, confusing, and painful bond, but it's the heart of why she still carries on in this world. At certain times in her life, she publishes other people's books, and has taught literacy to refugees and lectured on art appreciation and literature. While peaks and oceans are her retreat as an outdoorswoman, her home is wherever her furbaby is. Her poodle cross is Samwise to her Frodo.

Beatrice Wong

Beatrice Wong is a transgender outsider from Hong Kong with a lifelong struggle with mental issues, and lifelong delusions of being an artist. A failed filmmaker with just one work, a documentary short about her transition also titled *From Beavis (M) to Beatrice (F)*, she is able to sneak into screenings at LGBT festivals. Beatrice is now working as a research assistant in gender studies and is a hobbyist stand-up comedian. Zero significant awards but glad to be breathing after dosing herself with an excess of chemicals. This is her first published piece of writing.

Simon Wu

Simon Wu is an experienced writer—his plays have been performed in Hong Kong and London. In Hong Kong, by major theatre groups including The Hong Kong Repertory Theatre and Seals Players. In London, at Soho Theatre, Greenwich Theatre, Oval House, and Tara Arts. He has also been a Royal Court writer. His play *Oikos* has been published by Oberon Books. Three of his co-written radio plays have been broadcast on the BBC World Service. His short film, *Merry-Go-Round*, was nominated for Best Local Film in the Wood Green Independent Short Film Festival and screened at the British Film Institute in London.

Alistair Yong

Alistair Yong is an aspiring Malaysian writer who reads more than he should and writes less than he ought to. When he was writing his story for this anthology, he was still mending his broken heart. He sincerely dedicates his story to failed relationships, to those who have endured the heavier burden of painful breakups, to those suffering from depression, and finally, to those who are struggling with substance abuse.

CPSIA information can be obtained
at www.ICGtesting.com
Printed in the USA
FSHW020706300320
68616FS